Never Hug a Belly Dancer
and
99 Other Meditations
For Men

⊕

by
Toby Hill

Published by

IN HIS STEPS PUBLISHING
6500 Clito Road
Statesboro, Georgia 30461 (U.S.A.)

ISBN: 978-1-58535-201-2

Printed in the United States of America on acid-free paper.

Dedication

It's 12:20 a.m., and my wife, Anna Lee, and I have just finished seeing a movie on pay-per-view. As I sat in my glider-rocker in our small brick home, I watched as she came into the den where the TV is and began spreading her Christmas wrapping paper out all over the floor. She stooped on her knees and with tape and scissors in hand, wrapped presents as we watched the movie. Somewhere along the way, Anna Lee completed her wrapping and slipped up on to the couch where she finished the movie between moments of quiet and peaceful sleep. This is a scene which I have witnessed now for at least 43 years.

Anna Lee Carter Hill, my wife, is an untouchable. She is beloved by all. I share her with our three children and their families. I share her with our church family and all our many friends. She loves Christmas and will spend a lot of money each year trying to find the "perfect" gift for those she loves. We have traveled together to many parts of the world, but when all is said and done, she dearly loves to return to her mountain house where she was raised, near Asheville, North Carolina.

Over the years, she has opened up her home to all sorts of people. Our wonderful nephew, Kevin, lived with us for awhile. We had a foster child, and four different families that we had met overseas living with us off and on. She not only welcomes each stranger into her home, but immediately treats them as family.

Anna Lee and I are best friends. Another thing we did tonight was watch the UNC (University of North Carolina) basketball team win another game. Once upon a time, a long time ago, we took turns standing in line for basketball tickets on the Chapel Hill campus—lining up early in the morning and trading off when we had to go to class, just so we could get our favorite seats right under the basket in old Carmichael Auditorium. We were high school sweethearts. We met at a church camp when we were both fifteen, and have become inseparable. We seldom tire of each other's company. We were married while we were still in college, and have moved ten different times. She is the modest matriarch for our three adult children and seven grandchildren. We have truly been blessed by God to have Anna Lee in our lives.

     Now, almost fifty-years later, we are still each other's best friend. There is really nothing left to say about Anna Lee Carter Hill. My prayer would be that everyone could find that person in their lives who is their perfect match—their greatest love of all.

✝

Contents

☩

Introduction

What lies ahead are 100 short meditations that hopefully will relate to men. They are not written necessarily to be read in any particular way. They may be read one at a time, or the entire collection could be read in just a few minutes. The hope is that each meditation will give the reader pause for reflection. Perhaps that is the subtle difference between a meditation and devotion. Devotions are written to inspire; meditations are written to encourage reflection and self examination. There is little attempt to order these meditations in any particular way. They can be read pretty much in the order they were written.

There are a few things to consider before you begin to read. First of all, God is referred to as "Him." No apologies, but these are written for guys. Secondly, there may be some language in these meditations that might seem a little inappropriate. No apologies, but these are written for guys. Also, most of our friends know my wife as "Anna", but I refer to her by her southern name, "Anna Lee." No apologies, that's what I call her, and I have known her longer than anyone else. Finally, there are no footnotes or sources quoted. There really are not many original thoughts anywhere anymore, and most of what I have written about has been absorbed from hearing way too many sermons and reading way too few books. Also, I reflect and pray a lot. I have been influenced by C.S. Lewis, and one or two others that I cannot think of right now. There is, however, no plagiarism here. Just ideas and impressions that have been worked out in my own mind. As a great preacher that I know often says, "Every Blessing" upon you as you read these meditations. And, by the way, have some fun with them too!

Toby Hill
March 2010

Cutting the Grass With God

Grass cutting is a great release for me. I can get on a riding mower and, before long, my mind is a long way away from whatever is going on in my daily life. Last week I was cutting about two acres and I was thinking about God. I could have been thinking about our children and grandchildren, about college basketball, politics, or planning a new deck that I want to build, but last week I was thinking about God. I'm not much into quoting the Bible, but somehow it seems to me that the first four words of the scriptures are pretty important. They are "In the Beginning God..." So what I was thinking about was that if those first four words are to be believed, then all bets are off. If we believe that God is God, then anything is possible.

I am not sure that I always believe that God is God. If I really did, then maybe I should not be so interested in sports and decks and playing golf with a regular foursome every Friday. If I really believed that God is God, then would I not be a missionary in Africa or some kind of zealot out on the street preaching at the top of my lungs . . . But after some thought and experience, some things kind of make sense to me.

First of all, if we observed the world and those around us, it is just as easy to believe that God exists as it does to believe that God does not exist. Secondly, if God is God, then God can never be understood; God can only be experienced. Finally, God probably gets great joy out of seeing us happy and living well and liking sports and lawn work, and God is also saddened by the way we often screw things up. Perhaps we should give God a chance to allow us to experience His presence. Not by being any different than we are, but by looking out for God's presence in our lives.

If you've ever hit a golf ball 250 yards down the fairway, you sometimes don't see the ball when it lands. You go and look for it. If you are fixing up a house or getting ready to paint, you don't always see problem areas immediately—you have to look for them.

Today I did a crossword while I was waiting for my car to be washed and my oil changed. I did not see the answers immediately, I had to look for them. Maybe we should take some time just to look for God, even if we are not sure that God is there. It may be that we will find Him in our own unique way and that God will be very comfortable with who we are. It could be that by searching for

God, we will also understand that it's O.K. to be just a guy who likes to do lots of different kinds of stuff.

If God is God, He probably can deal with us just the way He finds us. Let's spend some time looking for God.

March Madness

Here's the deal: my lovely wife, Anna Lee, is in the den captivated by a college basketball game. Is it a game between our beloved alma mater and our fiercest rival? Nope. Is she watching a national championship game that may go into overtime? Not at all. My dearest is watching a first round NCAA tournament game between two teams that she had scarcely heard of three weeks ago. You see, she has money on the game. She's a bracketologist. A day or two ago, she took great care to fill out a bracket and send it along with $5.00 to a mutual friend who is running the pool. She is fully intending to win the whole thing along with the hundred or so dollars that goes to the winner.

Why is she so engaged with these two teams? There are two reasons. First, she made a decision to fill out the brackets. Secondly, she has a personal investment. These two dimensions have everything to do with our spiritual lives. First, we have to make a decision to play . We have to decide that we are going to give God the opportunity to work in our lives. That decision is made differently by each person, but it is fundamental to our spiritual journey. Secondly, we have to make an investment. We make that investment by our prayer life, our worship life, our study, and listening to God's call to be honest with ourselves about ourselves. What happens then, is that we become engaged with God, just like Anna Lee is engaged with those two teams she knew so little about 3 weeks ago. I don't know what she is so worried about. I've made my picks, and I'm a lock to win the whole thing!

What kinds of decisions and investments do we need to make in order to become engaged with God?

Going Out to Dinner With a Dead Man

Anna Lee and I went out to eat last weekend and ran into a couple from our old neighborhood. We were waiting in the lobby, and we had been given one of those disc-like things that glows and hums when it's your time to eat. I've never been too sure about what to do with those devices. Putting them in your pants pockets is probably not very appropriate. Any way, back to the couple from our old neighborhood. A mutual friend had died just a few weeks ago. This man was much closer to the other couple than to us. To them, he was at least as close as family, maybe more.

The man in the restaurant lamented about how much his old friend would be missed. Everyone who dies isn't always missed; at least to the point that there is an emotional hole left in the lives of a great many people. Those that are missed greatly seem to have one thing in common. Almost universally, those who are missed the most when they die are those that genuinely care very little about themselves and a great deal about others.

We can all remember those special children of God who were givers, not takers, listeners, not talkers, and who were willing to invest themselves in the lives of others. Also, we might profit by reflecting on how these special people ended their journey which had been respected by so many. Most likely they way they lived their lives was not by accident.

Checking the Weather Channel

The Weather Channel was on the other day. It was Sunday, and the announcer said something to the effect that in a certain part of the country, if you were planning on going to church, that the weather was going to be good. I almost did a double-take. How long has it been since I have heard any mention of "Church" in the media? Even on the Hallmark Channel, going to church is not mentioned with any frequency at all. Most people in our society seem to look at going to church as some kind of antiquated behavior that they really don't understand and grudgingly accept because they figure in a few years all of those who attend church will be dead and gone, and the empty buildings will become nursing homes or unique restaurants.

We go to church. It is a habit that we have grown to love. We have been going to church at the same place for almost 30 years. We love our church (sounds kind of corny, really!), and our church is changing. It is getting smaller and older. Fewer people come and, those that do, are getting a little long in the tooth.

Not long ago we had a younger couple from the neighborhood begin to attend services. They are a blended family and for a while they were kind of down on their luck with employment and health problems. Our church helped them out some and, after a few months, they had landed back on their feet.

Last week, during one of our services, it came time for the children's sermon. The children from this family went up to the front of the church for the lesson and while they were up there, it occurred to me that this family had evolved from one which needed our church to one that the church needed. At one time they needed the assistance and stability our church offered their family. Now our church needs the youth, exuberance and energy that they can offer. In many ways, this paradox is a metaphor for our relationship with God. It is interdependent. We need a relationship with God that allows us to lead our lives in the most fulfilling and abundant way. And God, though all powerful, needs for us to use our relationship with Him so that His kingdom, His way of having us live, can be shared by others.

It might be worthwhile to take a minute or two to think about how we need God in our lives and how God needs us so that others might know Him.

Overheated

Not long ago, we drove the car into the driveway and my wife said, "What is that steam coming up from under the hood?" I said, "Oh, Crap!" or something like that. Like the good husband that I am, I opened the hood of the car, inspected the situation, and proclaimed that I knew what the problem was. "It's the top heater hose that has a leak. I can fix it myself!"

Later that evening, a friend who knows a lot more about automobiles than I do, stopped by and I asked him to look at the car. After some inspection, he determined correctly that the problem was that the radiator had a small crack in it and needed to be replaced. We ordered the radiator from the internet and my friend replaced it. The problem was now corrected.

So often in our lives we seek the quick fix and focus on surface level problems. We fail to examine the depth or complexity of our situations, and try to "patch things up" rather than dealing with the reality that many of the problems with which we deal are derived from deeply held issues that we have been unwilling to face. I wanted the problem with my car to be a heater hose because that would be an easy problem for me to fix.

Perhaps we should examine our own personal issues and how we want them to be resolved in any easy, surface level manner, instead of the more fundamental changes that we need to ask God to help us make in our own lives.

⊕

In a Zone

Would you rather be a godly man, or a man of God? Think of the difference. A godly man lives his life in such a way that he tries his best to be the good man that God expects him to be. He is faithful to his wife, saves his money, attends church, and is a good parent who instructs his children regarding their spiritual lives. A godly man takes on the task of doing what he believes God would have him do. A man of God, on the other hand, does not try to do the right thing as much as be the right person. A man of God, once he has established a genuine relationship with God, cannot remember a day when he did not focus on God and yearn for an encounter with him. A man of God does not try to do what he thinks God would have him do. He is lead instead by the Spirit of God Who dwells within.

It's kind of like when a ball player is "in a zone." With the man of God, there is no spiritual "to do" list. There is however, a spiritual compass that points the way to the encounters God has in store for him.

Maybe we should take a minute and reflect on the degree to which we are guided by our spiritual compass.

☩

We All Need Prilosec

I just came in from watching TV with Anna Lee. For a late night snack, I ate pecans—fairly fresh and recently shelled. I should have had just a handful, but I ate and ate and ate. Now, I know I will regret it in just a few minutes when I go to bed.

As with most poor decisions, mine was made, not on head knowledge, but on impulse and desire. Each day we are faced with all those little decisions that will determine, "in so many ways," the quality of our lives. We cannot depend on information alone to lead us down the right path. Most of us have pretty good head knowledge about how to handle our money, how to take care of our health, and how to honor and care about those we love. If we are honest, though, all of us have done really stupid things when it comes to our money, our health, and our relationships. We must consider those elements of our personality which allow us to defy logic and knowledge and make really poor decisions. Is it immaturity, perceived immortality, or just arrogance? It might be that the more we humble ourselves, the more likely we are to make good choices in our lives. Most poor choices are self-centered ones. Most good choices are made with the good of others in mind, but they are also good for us in the long run.

Maybe we should reflect and consider the way we make the choices which guide our lives.

☩

That God Awful Truck

Our son in law, David, is a good man with a good heart. We could not have asked for better. But David has one problem—his truck. At David and Angie's home (Angie is our youngest daughter), there's an old yellow truck which for years has migrated through David's family. The truck has arrived at its most recent resting place—their driveway! It has only three good tires and is covered with a coat of pollen. The truck will not crank, and Angie believes it should be sold or scrapped. David, however, says no! He remembers the truck from years gone by. The truck is like a member of his family.

How easy it is to become emotionally involved with material things. We honestly believe that there are certain things that we could not bear to lose, until we do. Then, a giant hurricane or tornado or fire destroys what we have in a very few minutes, and what do we discover? Generally, we discover that those things really did not matter much at all.

Perhaps we should reflect about our relationship with things before they are acquired, not after they are gone. We are at our best when our happiness depends solely on the strength of our relationships, not on the quantity of our stuff. Just ask those who have lost everything. Let's think about what we would do if we suddenly lost all of the stuff in our lives.

Piling Up Pine Straw

In many religions, including Christianity, we are told that we should treat others as we would like to be treated—The Golden Rule. Perhaps we should consider how we would really like to be treated, and that would give us a good idea of how we should treat others.

I was unloading some pine straw from my truck this afternoon, and my neighbor across the street coincidentally chose that time to come to the street to get his mail. He strongly suggested that I should put the pile of pine straw a little further down the street instead of in front of his driveway. Of course, the truck was almost completely unloaded by this time. I looked over and it seemed to me that the pine straw was really not in front of his drive, and I said nicely, "I really think you can get out without too much trouble." He went back inside without saying a word.

Now, did he treat me the way he would like to have been treated? Probably not. Did I treat him the way I would have liked to have been treated? Well, no. Neither of us were mean-spirited, but neither of us had the other's best interest at heart.

Having the other person's best interest at heart is the crux of the Golden Rule. But that alone is not enough. We should also try to make the other person feel special.

My golf partner does this each time we play. Part of his game is trying to be sure that everyone else playing with him feels special and is having a great time, regardless of the score.

Don't we all like to have others take our best interest at heart? Don't we like to feel as though we are somehow special in the eyes of others? Perhaps we should return the favor. Let us think about whether we take the time not only to treat others well, but to treat them as if they are special children of God.

☩

Finally Growing Up

Anna Lee and I have three wonderful adult children—two daughters, Christy and Angie, and one son, Brian. Often, when we are discussing their situations, especially when we think they might be having problems, I will say somewhat dramatically, "Don't worry, he is a grown man" (or "woman", as the case might be).

Do you ever wonder what it means to be a "grown man?" Even in my sixth decade, I often feel like a little boy or a young adult. I think we all do for most of our lives. Being a grown man might mean realizing that no one else is going to take out the garbage unless you do it. And after you do it, no one is going to say, "Man, you did a great job with that kitchen trash bag!" Being a grown man also means that we have come to understand the reality of the passage of time. We know that our children will grow up. We know that the oil in our car will get dirty. We know that interest will compound. Grown men are really growing men. They come to realize that mind, heart, and souls will erode if they are not constantly challenged, stretched, and reflected upon. "If we don't use them, we lose them" applies to more of our makeup than we generally want to admit. Grown men figure this out.

What areas of our lives need to be challenged, stretched, and reflected upon?

☩

When to Sell Short

Several years ago our house flooded. The insurance company paid to have it repaired. When the repairs were completed, the contractor told me that I should sell the house right then when it looked its best. He had correctly figured out that it was kind of a money pit. We did not sell right then, but probably should have.

How do we know when to give up on someone or something? Timing is important. We need to know when to quit on a job, a car, an investment, a diet, or even a house.

Are there some things we cannot or should not ever give up on? Perhaps our kids, our families, our faith, our church, to name a few. How do we know when to say, enough is enough?

I have a friend who says, "When the horse you are riding expires, dismount." It may be that when staying with an endeavor too long begins to bring harm to others or defies logic, then we should consider discontinuing it. It also may be that when we quit at something simply to satisfy our own needs, we should think that situation through very carefully before we make a change.

If we pray and meditate seriously, concerning our circumstances, we may still not know what to do. We very likely, however, will learn what it is that is motivating our desire for change. Once we figure that out, our decisions become a little easier to make.

What truly motivates us when we make important decisions?

✠

There's No Quitting in Football

Over the last few days, I have been working on a presentation that I am going to make later in the week. Just as I was finishing it, I ran into a small problem that kept me from completing my task. I will finish tomorrow morning, but I am frustrated to no end. I want to finish what I start, not so much for myself, but I know others are depending on me.

How many times were we either told as children, or have told our own, that "if you start something, you can't quit"? Young athletes often try to play football or soccer or basketball and realize, about half way through the season, that they do not like the sport. Most parents make them stick it out. How much more important is it to finish what we start when we are dealing with personal and spiritual matters. We cannot raise children for five years and then quit.

How can we seek the nature of God in our lives, only to

stop before we have experienced the incredible peace and joy that awaits us? Finishing does not always mean getting to the end.

We have a friend whose brother ran a marathon and cramped up in the last mile and really did not finish. But were the first twenty-five miles run in vain? I think not. Our spiritual life is more of a journey that is never finished in our lifetime. But by never reaching the destination, but continuing the journey, we may well finish what we started.

Let's think about those journeys in our lives that we will never really want to finish.

⊕

Dinner With the Daughters

It never hurts to reflect on those occasions when we are really the happiest. Tonight our daughters and their families came over and had dinner with us. Sitting there with our family around the dinner table, I realized just how happy I was at that moment. One of my college professors once said that happiness comes when our ideal selves—the person we most want to be—coincides with our real selves—the person we are at that time. Tonight, it seemed for me, my ideal self and real self were in harmony as I was being the grandfather that enjoyed seeing his children and grandchildren doing well.

When our ideal selves and our real selves are separated by great differences, the result is unhappiness and stress. Take for example the outdoorsman who is forced to work in a cubicle all day long, or the gregarious person that goes through the day never talking to anyone, or the man who values family time who travels and is often away from home.

We often hear about the "abundant life" that is offered through faith. That abundance is so clear when we are most comfortable with the person we have become. Consider our ideal selves and our real selves. How close together or apart are they?

Owning Rather Than Renting

Anna Lee and I have had a good deal of experience as landlords, most of it bad! Generalizations regarding most groups of people are typically very dangerous, but we have found that, on occasions, those who rent are not as concerned regarding the property for which they are responsible as those who own.

One time we had a renter whom we believed used our apartment as a depository for stolen property. Another time, our son, Brian's, rental was vandalized by drug dealers trying to collect on a bad debt. We really know how to pick um! We have had some wonderful tenants, but they have been few and far between.

Perhaps we should reflect on whether we are renting our spiritual lives or owning them. If we are owners of our spirituality, we maintain it through prayer and meditation. We pay attention to it by recognizing God's presence in our lives. We improve it by study and worship. And we invest in it by making ourselves available to God's call upon our lives. If we are renters, we are temporary custodians who do not feel the responsibilities and joys of ownership. When we own our spiritual lives we claim it, and most importantly, we pay a price for it and pay that price joyfully.

Are we renters or owners of our spiritual lives?

☩

Beer and the NFL

My brother in law, Bill, dies tonight. My sister called, not long ago, and told us that he would be dead within twenty-four hours. He is 78 and has had Alzheimer's disease for three years. It has been full-blown for a year now. His death will be a relief to him and those who love him. Bill was just a good guy. He loved the NFL (National Football League), loved a good cold beer, and took care of his family. He was a devout Christian man. He took care of my mom when it was not so easy to do so. We traveled with Bill several times to Europe and Jamaica.

You learn a lot about a person when you travel with them. Bill was one of the best. I told my sister, in our conversation, that she should not feel guilty about the relief and closure she will feel later on, perhaps in the morning. In many ways, Bill has been dead for a long time before he drew his final breath. He drew the short straw. He was overtaken by the dreaded disease like a child playing pleasantly in the surf and turns around only to see a giant wave rushing down to knock him off his feet and roll him over and over it its wake.

People of faith do not fear death; they only fear dying.

Taking Time to Measure

Anna Lee and I are huge college basketball fans. We pull for our alma mater, a perennial national powerhouse that, over forty -years ago, we used to yell for from choice seats just underneath the basket in the arena on our college campus. Here we are, all this time later, still living and dying on every shot. This week we won one game by a basket and lost a game by a basket. From the comfort of our living room, I screamed and cheered and beat my fist on the table and did everything I could to pull my team through. My actions were filled with emotion and laced with very little impulse control.

Most of the time, in the real world, our actions should be more measured. I like that term—measured—because it implies consideration and reflection. It is OK to impulsively yell for your favorite team, but as men, we should be more measured in our response when dealing with the people with whom we come into contact every day. Our wives, children, friends, co workers and perfect strangers deserve the respect that a "measured" response offers; especially if an emotional outburst or an impulsive reaction to a person or situation would result in hurt feelings and closed communications.

It takes a powerful man to understand when a measured, mature response is called for and how much good it can do. Remember those times when our actions have not been measured and what we could or should have done differently.

The Size of Your Bladder

Every once in a while, I will have to travel with people whom I don't know very well at the beginning of the journey. By the end of the trip, we wind up becoming very familiar with each other. Spend some time on the road with others and sometimes you find out more than you really want to know about your traveling companions. You learn what they like to eat, how fast they like to drive, what sort of music they listen to, and how big or small their bladders are. If the trip is long enough, you will also learn about their children, their hobbies, and even, God forbid, their love life.

"Companions" is really a great word. It can mean so many different things. A companion may mean someone that you really don't care for, but must journey with. A companion could be a teammate or a soul mate. A companion often is a family member or a very close friend.

When we think about it, those that we choose as our companions, in many ways define who we are. Our best days are the ones when our companions are those whom we love and respect, and who love and respect us.

Reflecting on the quality of our companions might bring us to a closer understanding of the quality of our lives. Let's reflect upon who would call us their companion.

☩

Sick and Tired of Mission Statements

I am not sure about this, but I bet I am not the only person to be getting sick of mission statements, vision statements, and the listing of core values. The problem with the exhausting process of coming up with these three operational concepts is that they are most often not very genuine reflections of what our core values actually are. Wouldn't it be refreshing to have a business declare that their core value is "making more money", or "increasing our market share", or "raising our stock price", or "putting our competitors out of business?" How about the core value of a department or branch being stated as "guarding our own turf?"

We won't be seeing statements like these posted in the lobbies of many businesses. It may be that, personally, we really are not sure what our core values are. Perhaps our core values change as we mature—sometimes for the better, and sometimes for the worse.

Reflecting on the true nature of our core values is best done by asking three specific questions. The first is, "what thoughts preoccupy my time"? The second is, "what do I actually do during each day?" And finally, "where do I spend my money?"

Consider these three questions—that will give us a good idea of what our core values actually are.

⊕

Stuck in Traffic

This week we made a quick trip to Florida to see my sister, Laura, and our two nephews, Mike and Stephen, and our niece, Susan. As I said, it was a quick trip, but a good one. We had a chance to visit and had a nice dinner over at Mike's house. His wife, Karen, and son, Andrew, were great hosts. Stephen and his wife, Angie, and their two children, Amanda and Christopher, showed up. Susan came alone, and it was great to see them all.

Now, have you got all of that genealogy straight? Good,

but it really is not too important to the point of this story. I love my family, but I hate Florida! Too many times in the past have we been down there when something terrible has happened. Most of the time it's the weather. Once, we even lost a relative for two weeks after a storm. Another story for another time. Suffice it to say, this time was no different. On the way home, as we crossed the state on I-10, traffic came to a complete stop. I started to fidget and look up the road about 200 yards, and saw some tractor-trailer trucks getting off at an exit. That was all I needed. I got into the far right lane, got off the interstate, and started looking for another way home.

Our friend, Mark, who had gone down with us, got the GPS out of the glove compartment, and we actually did OK. We got back onto the interstate further up the road and came home with little problem. Anna Lee told Mark, however, that I was much more comfortable moving and searching for an alternate route than I was just sitting in traffic. She is right. I am like that.

In a way, that's like our spiritual journeys should be. We should be moving, even if we are lost and discouraged and searching for God, rather than just being stopped where we are. We should always be searching for God. We will never understand God, but we can only hope to feel His presence. How in the world can we feel God's presence if we have stopped searching for Him? We are just sitting in that spiritual traffic jam, hoping things will clear up.

By the way, when we got back onto the interstate, ten miles or so up the road, nothing was coming up the road behind us. Everyone who stayed behind was still stuck in traffic.

What are we doing to keep ourselves from getting stuck in our spiritual journey?

Trying to Steal Software

I just installed some new software on my computer. I tried my best to figure out a way not to have to buy it. I looked for imitations. I tried to use some that a friend our families had recently purchased. I tried to get the software for free. No such luck! So, tonight, Anna Lee and I went to the local office supply and I sucked it up and spent a good deal of money to purchase the real thing. It is interesting that, once I made that commitment and got the software home, I had it booted up in a matter of minutes. I am using it now.

In many ways, this technological story is analogous to our relationship with God. We realize that we need that relationship, but we try our best to avoid it. We look for imitations, maybe some type of self-help course. We try to use the faith of our friends or families and we quickly learn that, although the faith of others is to be admired, studied, and sometimes imitated, our relationship with God is personal and individual—it must have our own product-code on it. We also try to establish a relationship with God that is free of charge. That doesn't work very well either. Although God does not demand that we follow a strict set of rules, He convicts us in our heart with regard to the tasks to be performed, the lifestyle to be lead, and the relationships to be healed. This conviction really is much better than the software that was booted up just a few minutes ago.

Our relationship with God will not make us perfect all of the time, but our relationship with Him, once accepted, will anchor and guide our lives for eternity.

Is our relationship with God really guiding and anchoring our lives?

We Need Merry Maids

Have you ever cleaned up a house or apartment after someone has moved out? We have one rental property that is often more trouble than it is worth. This week we have been cleaning it up in order to have it ready for the next renters. What a mess.

You can learn a lot about a person when you clean up behind them. We can tell what those who were there last ate, drank, watched on TV, and wore to work. We also know how much they valued their own self-respect by the way they left the property in which they lived for the last few months.

It might not hurt us to consider whether or not we are leaving a mess when we move from place to place, or when we disconnect from others whom we have associated with.

I believe that God's will is for us to leave the places we visit and the people we encounter better off than they were the first time we showed up. What a powerful message and witness to our lives it would be if all of those with whom we have come into contact remember us as being positive, helpful, restorative, and nurturing. What a wonderful legacy that would leave when we moved away, in one way or the other, from wherever we are right now.

Are we leaving behind a physical or emotional mess for others to clean up once we have moved on?

✠

My Diet

Today I had a bad eating day. I need to lose weight and generally eat in a more healthy fashion. Not today. In the morning I had a full breakfast. My excuse—I was eating out with some men friends from church. At lunch I ate a big, fast food hamburger. My excuse—I was in a hurry to get my granddaughter home for her nap. To rationalize this 800 calorie entrée, I ordered some yogurt as a side dish instead of fries. I never ate the yogurt. At dinner more of the same. This time it was not so much what I ate but more the quantity of the meal. No small portions for me. Now the problem is not lack of information. I could probably come pretty close to counting the calories and the salt content of all my food for the day. My actions are more determined by my will and believing subconsciously that I am immune from the consequences of poor eating habits. I know better, I just have not made the emotional decision to do the things that I should.

Why do I do what I should not do, and do not do what I know I should? That question has haunted man for centuries. When I reflect on this reality, I believe I make poor decisions because I do not let the Spirit of God completely control my life. I sure hope I do better tomorrow.

Let's take some time and think about the degree to which we are allowing God's spirit to direct our lives.

⊕

You're Still Away

I played golf today. As I was preparing to get into the golf cart, before we teed off on the first fairway, I checked the storage compartment in the cart for holes to make sure nothing would fall out. Then, I took my watch off my wrist, my pocket knife, my wallet, and my cell phone out of my pockets and put them in the little compartment for safe keeping. When we mercifully finished 18 holes, I carefully searched for each item and retrieved them from the cart. All of my things were there, and so I stuffed them back into my pockets and put the watch back on my wrist. Sounds exciting doesn't it? As we drove home, I started thinking about how in our lives we often need to rid ourselves, even temporarily, of much of the excess stuff we carry around in order to play our game of life more effectively. This stuff can be material and personal. Getting rid of certain things we once thought we never could do without can be immensely freeing. Try giving it away, that's even better. Also, dumping some of our relational "stuff" like jealousy, bitterness, fear, and conceit can be just as freeing.

What about all the material and emotional "stuff" in our lives that we need to dump out of our pockets and leave in the cart, perhaps forever?

☩

Send It Back to China

What a day. Up early and off to pay off a guy who is helping me with some repairs. Went to work for a little while and then to see my grandson's basketball game. So far so good, right? No, just before the ballgame, Anna Lee tells me the car is overheating again after a new radiator was installed last week. I figured the worst. I would have to send the radiator that was purchased over the internet back to Hong Kong or God knows wherever I bought it from! After the game, I came home and opened the hood and started checking out the radiator. I looked and looked for the problem. When my friend came to help me with the car, he found a simple hose clamp which had come loose, and it took ten minutes to fix it. I assumed the radiator was the problem because I expected the worse. My pessimism got in the way of reality.

How often does that happen in our daily life? We expect the worse and look for the worse, and what happens? We miss the joy!

Perhaps we should remember that God actually wants us to live abundantly. What we miss so often is that the abundant life has everything to do with our attitude and very little to do with the radiator. By the way, Anna Lee took my truck out while we were working on the car and had a "small" accident in the Wal-Mart parking lot. Another story for another day.

Have there been times when our pessimism has contributed to our missing the joy in our lives?

⊕

Liar, Liar, Pants on Fire!

Someone lied to me today. A friend's mother told me years ago not to use the word "lied", but to substitute "misinformed" in its place. So I will give this person the benefit of the doubt and say that someone misinformed me today. It was a business issue, and I found out later that the employee had been instructed not to disclose certain information to their customers. But I was not told, "I am sorry, sir, but I cannot disclose that information." Instead I was misinformed.

C.S. Lewis would call that kind of behavior, "seeking comfort instead of the truth." His conclusion is, that when we seek comfort in place of truth, we find neither. We should examine our lives to look for those instances where comfort seems truly more important that truth. Perhaps our financial situation could use a little truthful examination. Perhaps our parenting skills or our commitment to our community should be more closely examined. Perhaps we should recognize the truth about how much time we spend enhancing our spiritual lives or how we really treat others. Can we be truthful about our personal habits?

Facing the truth is tough sometimes, but in the long run it is the only way to live. By facing the truth, we will eventually find comfort. Maybe we should spend some time examining what are the areas in our lives where we really need to face the truth.

✛

The Smartest Guy in the Room

I have always had a problem in that I, from time to time, consider myself the smartest guy in the room. If there is a more obnoxious attitude, I don't know of one. It took me a long time to realize that there is quiet a difference in being intelligent and being smart. Intelligence does one little good unless it is coupled with good, common sense. Too often, at least in my own personal situation, I am far more intelligent than smart, and that has proved troublesome over the years.

This idea of depending too much on one's own intelligence can especially be a problem when it comes to our faith journey. It is very difficult to make an intelligent case either for or against the existence of God. Believing in that existence really requires that we be smart and accept this reality on faith. It is only when we understand that we can't understand that we begin to understand.

We saw a church service on *YouTube* not long ago where people went across the stage with cardboard signs. On one side of the cardboard was written a description of themselves before they had a relationship with God. Maybe something like "unfaithful." On the other side of the sign was a description about how their life had changed since they had become serious about their spiritual journey - something like "loving husband." The service was called "Cardboard Confessions." If I were writing my own cardboard confession, it would say on one side, "intellectual", and on the other side, "believer." There is a ton of difference in defining God and believing in him. As I have said before, this transformation all begins when we accept on faith and truly believe the four words

"In the beginning God..." It might not be a bad idea to get our copy of the scriptures, turn to the first page and read these first four words. If we can accept them, not with our intelligence but with a faith based on our own experience, then our spiritual journey begins, and we will be taken to places that we can only begin to imagine.

What would be on your cardboard confession?

✠

What Happens in Vegas
Can Cause Problems

We had a friend whose 18 year old son and his stepfather did not get along very well. Just before the young man was to go to college, there was an especially difficult conflict between the two. The mom asked a local church to allow the young man to stay for three weeks before he left town for college in an unused apartment that the church owned. Of course the deal was that the mom would check on the young man regularly, as would members of the church family.

This arrangement worked well for about ten days. Then the mom and step dad decided to take a long weekend for themselves in Las Vegas. Go figure! The young man got into trouble while the mom was gone. He was asked by the church to find other accommodations. It is not rocket science to determine that this young man needed someone to monitor his behavior.

Who monitors our own behavior? Have you ever had your scales in your bathroom break or come up with a dead battery? My guess is that when that happens you are like our family that eats more than we should when we don't weigh every day. Our spiritual life helps us monitor our own behavior. Some would say that spirituality inflicts guilt or fear and we obey the rules because we are told to. It is just as reasonable to believe that spirituality brings understanding about the Kingdom of God and our personal relation to him. Our faith journey allows us to experience an inner peace when we know behavior that is favored in the eyes of God is also that which is good for us—making us the complete person that God would have us become. That inner peace is the best kind of scale of all. It might do us good to reflect on what exactly motivates our behavior.

✠

Did Gandhi Go To Heaven?

Anna Lee and I are Christians. Being Christian is not as cool or accepted today as it used to be. To make matters worse, we are mainline Protestants. The mainline churches are the ones that a lot of people don't trust or don't relate to today. Most of them are losing members like crazy. Many Christians are going to the big, contemporary mega churches now and not to churches like ours.

One of the questions that Christians get asked often is about all of those good people who are not Christian or who never had a chance to become Christians. What happens to them?

When I was a younger person, I sat in a seminar with a guy who was supposed to know a lot about God. Someone asked him if Gandhi, the great Indian religious and political figure who led India to independence and believed in non violence, had gone to heaven. The man leading the seminar gave some kind of hokey answer about conversion at the end of life. I think he gave the wrong answer. If someone asked me if Gandhi went to heaven, I would have to say that I have enough confidence in God to let him work that out.

The next question by the skeptics usually is, "Then you don't have to be a Christian to go to Heaven?" The only way I could answer that is that I am not sure about anyone else, but for me, I must be a Christian to experience eternal life. Are those two answers in conflict? I don't think so because I have had a personal encounter with Christ. Therefore if I choose not to accept and worship him, then I reject him. That is not a good thing. I thought that if someone is reading these meditations it is important to know a little bit about the faith journey of the one doing the writing.

What would you say if someone asked you about your faith journey? It might be worth thinking about.

Having Lunch With God

Many Christians do something others think is kind of peculiar. They go to church and eat bread and drink wine and somehow that experience brings them closer to God. This worship experience is called Holy Communion, or the Eucharist, or the Lord's Supper.

Something occurred to me tonight that I should have realized long ago. If we truly believe that when we take the wine and bread we are actually partaking in the body and blood of Christ, then when we eat the bread and wine Christ actually becomes part of us at that moment. We are one body, and others should not be able to figure out which part of us is Christ and what part of Christ is us. A new person has been created by the joining of Jesus and our old selves.

It's like after we have lived with someone for years and years the union that is created takes on a life of its own. I remember when my father and mother celebrated their fiftieth wedding anniversary, the joy was not only in their love for each other, but it was just as equally in their pride over the "marriage", or union, they had created.

So it is with our relationship with Christ. Not only do we celebrate His love for us, and not only do we feel great joy when we express our love for him, the most important thing is the Union between Christ and ourselves. It is the Holy Union that most tells others about our relationship with Christ, not the two way connection on which we put most of our focus.

Maybe we should take a look at our own relationships with others that we love. What kind of union are we forming? Does that union take on a life of its own?

✠

Relax, He'll Be There

Today a man, whom I have known for a long, long time, went by a piece of rental property that we have to do some work for some new tenants. This man has fought his own demons for many years. I hope I have helped him with his struggles from time to time. I know he has helped me with my own. He told me when he would arrive to do the work. Shortly before it was time for him to go by, the tenant called and impatiently asked where he was. Although I didn't say it, I wanted to say, "I have known this man for thirty years. I've known you for about thirty minutes. Relax, he'll be there." I did not say it, I thought it, and perhaps I should have said it.

It occurred to me later that that thirty years relationship is a lot like God's relationship with us. He has known us forever. He knows whether or not we are dependable. He knows if we tell the truth, if we are faithful to our families, if we love one another. We don't need to con God about who we are. More importantly, regardless of who we are, He takes us where we are and starts working on us from that point. After all, he has "known us for thirty years, not thirty minutes."

Maybe we should reflect on the person that we have become that God knows so well. Who is that person, really?

☩

I Am the Hero

This week Anna Lee and I have been helping host a wedding party that has been visiting the U.S. from the UK. The bride is a daughter of old family friends. The family has come upon difficult times lately - so difficult that the bride's father was in the hospital at the time of the wedding. The groom is a nice young English man, and his family all came from England for the wedding. Many in our church reached out to the family in many ways. Anna Lee coordinated a wonderful meal and another friend hosted the bridesmaid luncheon. A family friend cooked the wedding cake, the church helped with lodging, and everyone chipped in to do as much for this family that we love as we could.

It fell to me to drive the church bus back to the airport for their return trip to England. On the way, everyone was so thankful and appreciative for our generosity, that is was difficult to know how to respond. To be honest, it felt good to be a hero. We had come to the rescue of these wonderful people and they thanked us over and over again. But when I look at these emotions carefully, I realize that feeling good about being a hero is really a negative, almost evil reaction. It runs to our motivation for doing the right thing. Do we serve because we want to be known as a good, kind and loving person, or do we serve because we are the children of a loving, kind God? It's often a tough call for me. I wish I did not like being a hero so much.

$$\maltese$$

Game Planning

I like football. Think about a situation where it is the beginning of the fourth quarter. You are ahead 16-10. You have the ball on your opponent's 47 yard line and it is fourth and a long one to go. What does the coach do? Well a lot depends on the situation. How is your running game? How is your defense playing? How is your punting game? All kinds of situations come into play. But the question boils down to how much field position are you willing to sacrifice by going for the first down, and how much are you likely to gain by punting?

This question of the balance of sacrifice and gain dominates our lives. How much time with our families do we give up in order to gain economic security? How many hamburgers should we give up in order to gain good health? How long should we allow our investments to mature before taking advantage of their worth to our well being? Life is a series of decisions that we make on the basis of balance between sacrifice and benefit. Unfortunately, we often apply this sacrifice/benefit formula to our relationship with God. We ask, "What will I have to give up if I accept the love of God in my life?" The answer is nothing. God does not require us to give up anything because he loves us just as we are.   Often, once we establish a personal relationship with God, our lives do change dramatically. But that change occurs not because God gives us a list of do's and don'ts, but because when we look at the world through God's eyes we see the world as he sees it. As a result, much of what we thought was real and important we come to understand is transient and trivial. How often do we think about how many things of value we sacrifice in order to gain things which really don't make much difference in the long run?

⊕

Our Rocks

We were in a meeting tonight and the subject of forgiveness came up. The group was only about 15 people, but they did not know each other very well. The son of one of the members in our group committed suicide not long ago. After the meeting, a few of us began to talk about experiences we had in common and this grieving parent was surprised to learn that another couple in the group had also gone through a terrible situation involving the death of their son. As we examined the group closely, we realized that almost every family unit represented had its own story to tell.

The world teaches us that image is everything. From the type of car we drive to the kind of makeup we put on our faces. We are told over and over again to not let others see us as we really are, but to hide the cracks in our lives behind a façade of material possessions. The truth is that we all have our own bag of rocks that we carry around. We are all human with faults. We have bad experiences and poor judgments, impulsive behaviors and our own personal nightmares. Life becomes real and exciting and deeply spiritual when we begin to share our true stories with one another. It is quiet a relief to realize that we are not the only ones who are flawed, and virtually everyone has the common experience of imperfection in one way or another. Not only is there a relief in realizing that it is OK not to be perfect, there is also a joy in learning of the great victories so many have had over so much tragedy and imperfection.

Do we have people in our lives that we can be "real" with?

First Aid

Yesterday I was working with a community group on a service project. I cut myself on an old fence and my hand started to bleed. A young lady there that I knew from Church asked if I needed a band aid. I really did and so I followed her over to her van for her to help me. As she was dressing my wound, we started a conversation about work, family, and all of the normal things those who know each other casually discuss. I realized that I knew her father when he was working. He had owned a local hardware store and had retired when the big box stores moved into town. I also remembered that she had had a paraplegic brother who had died, and then she continued her story by telling me about the loss of a second brother a few years later. As we concluded the treatment and the conversation, I told her how much her father was respected in our community and how we wished him well in his retirement years.

In just three or four minutes, we had grown from virtual strangers to connecting in a very meaningful way. She had ministered to my physical wound and I hope that I was able to minister to some of the emotional scars left over from the loss of her siblings. All it took was two children of God who gave of themselves to one another and asked for nothing in return. How often do we give of ourselves and ask nothing in return?

☩

Casual Sex

One result of our spiritual journey is that we eventually begin to have our world view shaped in new and exciting ways. God's desire for us to have an abundant life begins here on earth, and it begins by our understanding the difference between the spiritual view of the word abundant and the world's view of that same word. The world defines abundant in terms of quantity. The bigger the house, the car, the portfolio, the better off we are. (There is a difference when it comes to our wives. We seem to want them small.)

Think for a moment about the world's view of sex. The world tells us that the more we can get, the better we are. That thinking leads to our most overused and dangerous oxymoron— the term, "casual sex." The spiritual view of sex does not set limits on it (thank goodness). However, the spiritual view gives us parameters that help us deal with our sex life. The spiritual view of sex points us toward understanding it in terms of its effect on our relationships and responsibilities. There is nothing casual about those dynamics. We also know that sex occurring outside of those two parameters does have detrimental consequences, sometimes felt only years later. I know a very spiritual man who, from time to time, still has trouble dealing with his guilt about a one night stand that he had 20 years ago when he was a young married professional away on a business trip. It is doubtful that it ever occurred to him, on that lustful night years ago, that that one night stand would turn into an issue he would deal with for many nights to come.

How often do we take the time to consider that all of our actions affect our relationships and our responsibilities?

☩

Swamp Gravy

We saw a really good play this weekend. It is called *Swamp Gravy*. *Swamp Gravy* is folk theater, and its subject this year is family reunions. One of the lines in the play was, "nothing worth doing can be accomplished in one generation." I am not sure I totally agree with that statement, but it does give one pause to consider a very important question. How does the world see activity and success, and how does God see activity and success? We scamper from here to there with all sorts of technology designed to help us manage our time. We set long and short term goals, mileposts and outcome measures, but at the end of the day, much of what we have accomplished is temporal at best. God sees our activities as eternal and it would profit us to consider our daily lives in terms of, "What are we doing that will impact generations to come?"

Most of these, "eternal activities", revolve around our families, our creative lives, and our spiritual journeys. Yet the world does all it can to denigrate the family, place us in mind-numbing jobs, and expose us to a juvenile and intellectually hostile media, while at the same time minimizing the importance of spirituality. God's message to us is simply that we can do better than that. His desire is for us to live abundantly and that abundance begins here on earth, and the foundation for that abundant life lies in our doing those things that are important enough to impact generations to come—raising our families, creating a better world using our gifts and talents, and embarking on a spiritual journey that daily brings us closer to God.

Let's spend some time thinking about how many of our daily activities will really impact future generations.

☩

Always the Teacher

"Let me tell you one thing." If I am not careful I will start every other sentence that way. I am compelled to be instructive. I don't think I am showing off, I just feel like people need to know more than they do, and it seems to have fallen to me to tell them. What a pain in the rear attitude that is. I am trying to do better, to be more conscious regarding what I say. I am trying to be a better listener and not believe it is my right and duty to instruct every person I meet regarding every aspect of their lives. Don't churches and overly religious people often make the same mistake that I do? They want to instruct us, teach us the rules, and tell us what we need to do in every situation. We don't really need instruction, we need inspiration, acceptance, prayer, and an extended hand.

As a Christian, I believe that Christ, who was God, did not tell us what to do as much as offered Himself to us. As a Christian, I believe it is my responsibility to treat others, not only as I would like to be treated, but also I need to treat others as Christ has treated me.

I had better stop now, I am beginning to get a little too instructive. Let's reflect on where in our lives we need inspiration instead of instruction and how we might find it.

⊕

Making It Big

There comes some point in the lives of almost every man when he realizes that he is not going to make it to the "top." The self-help genre would say that that previous sentence is blasphemy. We should never give up on our goals. We will never reach our goals unless we raise the bar high.

Many of us have been in meetings were our objectives, or quotas, or profit potentials were set and we start immediately to try to meet these projections. Personally, we start careers expecting to reach an exalted professional status, and we are all encouraged to aim for the top. We are told that we should want our boss's jobs and that we all should reach our maximum potential, whatever that means. But at some point, the reality sets in. A tree can only grow so tall. There is room for only one CEO, President, and Board Chairs in our organizations. We only have room for one mayor in our cities, one principal in our schools, and one sales manager in our districts.

The reality is that after all of our hard work, the world sees us as just another average guy trying to take care of our family. Often, when we understand how the world really sees us, we get a little depressed, or angry, or lethargic. We slow down and put our lives on an emotional cruise control, or we turn to expensive hobbies, vices, and habits. We try lots of stupid things to take our minds off the world-view that we too easily accept, that eventually, we are to end up as only an average guy. When we first bought into the message that we will achieve great, great, worldly accomplishments, we made the mistake and vastly overestimated our worldly worth. At the same time, we have vastly underestimated our spiritual worth. The world sees us in only one dimension—the image of power and its ability to allow us to acquire a lot of stuff.

We know it is a "material world." The world denies the importance and, in many ways, even the existence of a spiritual dimension that dwells deeply within all of us. Once we tap into our own depth of spirituality, then the "spiritual sky knows no limit."

Maybe we should spend some time thinking about whether we truly accept the world's view of ourselves and then consider how God sees us.

Living With The Witch

It seems to me that tennis shoes and our tapping into our personal spirituality have a good bit in common. A very well known man was, at one time, caught in a trap. He had at first come to believe in God, and later became a well-known Christian spokesperson in his home country. He believed that his life should be as Christ-like as possible—even when he did not feel like it, which was often the case. He had promised an old friend that he would take care of his family if the friend was killed or injured in war, which he was. And so this man took on the responsibility of caring for his deceased friend's mother and sister. The mother turned out to be a pain in the rear, and this Christian man was urged over and over again by his friends to put her out of his house, in that she treated him so badly. He believed that it was his Christian duty to love and care for this woman, and so he decided to do so. He kept his promise to care for these women for over 30 years. By deciding to behave like a Christian, even though he did not feel like doing so, he became a great Christian teacher and lecturer, and has served as an inspiration to millions of spiritual seekers over the years. In other words, he "just did it", like the tennis shoe company says. That behavior is the key to our tapping into the spiritual dimensions of our lives.

When we don't feel like praying, or meditating, or studying, or opening ourselves up to God, we need to just start the process and act like we are doing it until we actually are finding greater and greater depths in our own spiritual journey. Somewhere in the Hebrew Scriptures it says, "I sought the Lord and he found me." It does not say, "I waited until I felt like it and then I sought the Lord."

What can we do to start our or reignite our spiritual journey when we don't feel like it?

Listening With Your Inner Ear

Life is a balancing act in many ways. Two of its dimensions that we must learn to balance are, "theory and practice." If we are too theoretical, we really are not much good to anyone.

There is the old saying that, "I asked a guy what time it was and he told me how to make a watch." You know the type. They are filled up with theory and cannot find their way home. Too much attention to practice also has its own liabilities. There are some who follow every rule and regulation. They will go around their elbow to get to their rear end if that is what the procedure's manual prescribes. They take months to make a decision that should take seconds because it is so obvious. They thrive on the trivial and ignore the elephant in the room.

To be successful in our world, we need to be practical enough to accomplish what is necessary, and theoretical enough to understand our mission and our options, and to look for creative approaches to get the job done.

Our spiritual lives require much the same balancing act. We cannot be so holy that all we do is pray and commune with the Holy Spirit. We cannot spend all of our time discussing the nuances of theology, or become so engrossed in the study of the scriptures that we ignore the world around us. On the other hand, we cannot be so practical that all we care about is doing what we think God wants us to do, and get so caught up in trying to live out our spiritual life that we fail to feel God's warmth in our hearts, and to be in awe of God's majesty. Our lives should not be isolated in a theoretical way, or totally immersed in the world in a purely practical way. Our lives should be lived out in the world, but insulated from it at the same time. If we strike that balance in this world, we can act as God wants us to, but always being conscious of the spiritual mystery of the faith that most of the world never experiences. It is that mystery that makes our faith holy. It is that mystery that makes our faith much more than life's little instruction manual.

Do we tend to be more theoretical or more practical? Are we too much of either one?

Listen To Your Wife

Anna Lee often talks about life being filled with circumstances that require us to choose between our desires and our duty.
As we seek God's will in our lives, it seems only too clear that for
God, "Life is Duty." When we consider this simple sentence carefully, we might be drawn to the conclusion that God's call on our
life leads us to a dreary and tedious destination where all we are
about is trudging though life being oh so serious about doing the
duty that God wants us to do. But as we feel God's presence running deeply through the sinews of our existences, we begin to understand and experience a corollary to the previous statement. Not
only do we realize that "Life is Duty", we also understand that
"Duty is Joy."

Our duty to God is His calling on our lives. When we allow the Holy Spirit to fill our lives, His light illuminates His will
for our lives. When we are in His will, we are doing His duty. This
is not the duty God requires, it is the duty we discover. There is no
greater joy than being in the will of God. There is no greater peace
than knowing that we are leading our lives in accordance with
God's plan for us. There is no greater revelation than realizing that
God's plan for our lives is for us to be at our best, to have a focus
on His will for us, and to discover our duty in God's world, and
make that duty our life's mission.

Have we ever felt God wills us in one direction, and we
find ourselves ignoring him and doing something else completely?

⊕

God and Barry Sanders

Barry Sanders was a great running back. Sometimes he ran the football and it seemed as if he was impossible to tackle. One day Barry Sanders did a very unusual thing. He retired in the prime of his career. If he had played a few more seasons, he would certainly have broken many of the records held by the best football players ever. So many sports reporters and fans tried to find the "real" reason for Barry's retirement. The world's view was that there was no way he would retire unless there was some hidden agenda that he would not disclose. As far as we know, he was not injured or chose to retire for any other reason than he defined success in his own terms.

At times we must define success for ourselves. That is not always so easy. Sometimes it is not only the world, but the expectations of our families or even those organizations like the church, that are supposed to be in the business of spiritual and personal guidance, that want to define success for us. God wants us to define success for ourselves. God wants us to be complete individuals and not robots, either in our worldly or spiritual lives. The great miracle of life is that we are who we are and there is no one else like us. That is part of what a personal relationship with God means.

How do we define success for ourselves, and what does it mean that there is no one else like us anywhere in the universe?

☩

The Tract On The Urinal

Today we went to visit a large and beautiful garden for a great day with some friends that we have not seen in over a year. Toward the end of the afternoon, my friend and I went into the restroom for one last stop before we began our trip home. When I stepped up to the urinal, there, placed just on top of the urinal in easy eye level, was a tract (a small brochure) on the four steps to salvation. I asked my friend if he thought that placing the tract on top of the urinal was effective evangelism. He just laughed and we washed up and left.

On the way home, I got to thinking about how demeaning leaving the literature on the urinal was to God. Our Spiritual life and our relationship to God is a sacred and deeply personal matter. I heard someone say that we should not put on the bumpers of our car those thoughts that are better placed in the depths of our hearts. Perhaps we should add, "tops of urinals", as an addendum to that thought. In all actuality, though, we should evaluate our lives in terms of identifying those aspects of our being and our daily routine that are sacred and personal, and should be treated as such. Our responsibilities to those sacred elements of our existence are much more important than our responsibilities to the less sacred and sometimes trivial aspects of our life. A little meditation on those parts of who we are, that are truly sacred, could help us all enormously.

☩

I'll Call

We used to play a lot of cards. My mother taught my sister and me how to play bridge by playing three-handed, while we all sat cross-legged on the bed. As I grew older, I played cards all night long in the basement of my dorm room, and watched many of my more well-heeled classmates win and lose what, to me, were enormous sums of money playing high stakes poker.

My wife and I made fast and lifelong friends over a card table when we were in graduate school. We would put the kids down and get out the cards, and we guys would take on the ladies in uproarious bridge hands. Actually, we still play once or twice a year with the same couple nearly 40 years and 8 grandchildren later.

Terms associated with playing cards have become a common part of our vernacular. I heard someone say once that for many politicians, positions on policy "trumps" personal behavior. Often we hear of people "playing the race card." It might be worthwhile to consider what "cards" we play in our daily lives. Do we play the "power" card, or the "gossip" card, or the "passive aggressive", or even the "stuff" card, in order to get our way or try to make ourselves look good in the eyes of others? There is no question that God plays the "love" card. God loves us, and we try to love God as best we can. God is truly playing with a full deck. What about us? Playing the love card should be the first card out of our personal deck, and the last card held that, when played, helps all who are playing the game. Playing the love card is very intentional and it always beats the other petty cards that the world expects us to play.

Perhaps we should consider what are the favorite cards that we play on a day to day basis.

⊕

A Phone Call From the Past

I just hung up the telephone after having a lengthy discussion with an elderly, but extremely intelligent and gracious lady. Basically, I, at one time, worked for her husband (now deceased), I am friends with her son, and her grandson works for the organization with which I am associated. There is a problem and she wants my help. During the conversation, I told her that our family was a better family because we had been associated with her family in one way or another for the past 30 years.

I began to reflect on the enormity of that statement. Will others who have rubbed up against our family be able to say the same thing about us 30 years from now? We also might reflect on all of the types of families that we claim as our own. We belong to work groups and community groups that could be considered families. There are church families, and we often hear of athletic teams as being a family. Are all of these families acting in such a way that people will say in the future that they were better off for having been a part of the family, or having been affected by them in some way?

The people of God are often referred to as a family. A fair question would be—are others better off by being a part of God's family? Also, are those outside of the family of God better off because the family of God exists? Tonight I will try to consider these questions as I reflect upon my day.

Two Views of Life

This morning I had the privilege of helping out in our food ministry at our church. My job there is to check people in who are coming for their monthly supply of groceries. It is a fairly simple process. We check their ID and their addresses, and move them inside to see a counselor. The idea is to do this while helping those who are coming in to maintain their dignity and sense of worth. What often helps me is the belief that there is a spark of divinity in each person. If we look hard enough (sometimes it is not so hard, actually), we can see an image of God in everyone we meet.

This evening, I also had the privilege of going to a banquet where outstanding students were honored for the work they had done this year. Four of these students had actually won a national championship. These students were not necessarily advantaged, most came from working class homes and had seen the importance of making good decisions, setting goals, and working very, very hard. It occurred to me that the image of God was also present in each of these young people.

Two groups of very different people had been encountered on my journey this day. The presence of God was reflected in the lives of each, even though they were miles and miles apart in where their lives had taken them.

How important is it to always try to look for the image and presence of God in each person that we encounter? We learn more about that person and we learn a great deal more about God. What image of God do others, especially our wives and children, see in us?

Thirteen Seats

Last week I was lucky enough to be invited to an award's banquet where a team of four persons was given an award for winning a national championship. Their supervisor told an interesting story. He said that over twenty years ago, he had been at a national convention where someone sitting close to him was given a national award. He said he counted the seats between himself and the award winner. There were 13 seats between them. He asked himself, "What is the difference in these 13 seats between this winner and me?" After some thought, he said that it occurred to him that great success can come when "our dreams become our expectations." I do not know if that phrase is original with him. But I do believe there is a powerful message in converting our dreams into our expectations.

But this thought can be extended. What about considering how powerful our lives would be if we allowed God's dreams for each of us to become our expectations for our own lives? God says that He dreams for us a life of abundance, love, healing, peace and joy. Often our expectations for ourselves are set so low by the world's standards. Perhaps we should spend some time in meditation and reflection trying to figure out how the dreams that God has for us can become expectations that we have for our journey on this earth.

☩

Who Am I, Exactly?

This is who I am. I have been blessed to have a wonderful wife and family. We are not perfect, but we are functional and we love each other. I have been blessed to have had a good education. I went to a good high school and three fine colleges. I have been fortunate to have been elected to public office three times. Again, I was not a great public servant, but I did not embarrass myself or my family. I am a committed Christian whose greatest personal sin is not rising to the full human potential that God has bestowed upon me. I also understand that Christianity is a very personal faith, and that perhaps our greatest corporate sin is refusing or relinquishing our relationship with Christ once we have personally encountered His love for us. Also, we have failed to understand that being judgmental, regarding those who have yet to have such an encounter, is not pleasing to God. I worry about the Church. I worry too much in general. I have wonderful friends. I am a pretty good writer, but do not have the self discipline to write as much as I should. I love college basketball and major league baseball. I can teach just about anything I can read and understand. I do not like conflict and often spend too much time trying to please others. Most importantly, I love my wife, Anna Lee, our children and our grandchildren more than life itself. That pretty well sums it up.

Maybe we should all write a paragraph that honestly says, "This is who I am."

✠

Long Hair and Curfews

When the discussion of raising children comes up, we often hear that parents have to "set boundaries" for their children. Setting boundaries conjures up images of an impatient dad staying up and watching the clock to see if his adolescent daughter comes in just one minute after her curfew. Or the same father having a fit because his son's hair has gotten too long for the father's tastes.

God help us if our kids get a tattoo! It may be that there is a problem with setting boundaries. The problem is that boundaries change. Curfews vary depending on the time available and circumstances. Fashion, music, and customs all change from generation to generation, and the boundaries that parents set change with them. Sometimes, by the time the third of fourth child comes on the scene, the parents are just too tired to enforce boundaries as vigorously as they did with their elder children. It might not be as important for fathers to set boundaries as it is for them to determine which boundaries they have inherited from the generations before them that are not ever to be changed. When we make that determination, we can begin to figure out which battles are worth fighting, and just possibly we can help save our children from what can be the horrible influence of modern culture.

A good meditation exercise is to reflect on what boundaries are non-negotiable. There may not be as many as we think.

☩

Football On a Saturday Afternoon

One of the non-negotiable boundaries, with regard to raising children that helps us become the kind of dads that God knows we can be, is to always put our family's needs above our own self interests. That does not mean that we should never play golf, or go fishing, or watch college football on Saturday afternoons. Putting our family's needs ahead of our own does refer to our patterns of behavior. Do we always watch college football on Saturdays when our children need our attention? Do we teach our children how to play golf and take time with them when we had rather be on the course with our friends? As parents, do we too often say "no" to the things we should say "yes" to, and "yes" to the things we should say "no" to? If our children want us to play with them in the middle of our favorite TV show, do we say, "not right now"?

Fast forward to a young teenager asking to spend the night with a friend that you might not approve of but you say yes because it will get them out of the house for a while. How do we as dads put the needs of our family ahead of those of our own? It is a question worth reflection.

☩

Do As I Do

Is it too simplistic to say that one non-negotiable boundary that men should have when raising their families is to lead by example? If we believe that what we say to our children is of little importance, and what we do in front of our children is of eternal importance, if we truly believe that, then the way we live our lives will change dramatically. The most dramatic change will be that we will begin to lead lives of self examination. We will pray each morning that God's Holy Spirit guides what we say and do during that day. But we will not have to examine each moment as it occurs and think about the enormous consequences of even our smallest actions. We will live not so much trying to model behavior by consciously thinking about every little thing we do, but more by experiencing each day. By focusing on God and his spirit, we will then be led to instinctively behave in terms of how our families will be affected by what we do and what we think—even when we are away from them. I find myself often trying to change my behavior by putting my actions under a microscope, instead of focusing on God and letting my behavior take care of itself.

Finally, we will end each day examining and reflecting on the best and worst parts of that day in terms of our relationship to God and our relationship to those we love. "Leading by example" may not be as easy as it sounds.

Tonight, let's look back on the degree to which we focused on God, and then on what we did today. Finally, check out the example that we have set for those who are looking up to us.

✛

Making a Bad First Impression

There is an old axiom in advertising that says, "You never have a second chance to make a first impression." I've never been particularly good at that. I tend not to be aware of the importance or significance of the situation. Sometimes, I am kind of out of it, and don't figure out what is really going on until later on. I have always admired those who can size up a situation immediately and not have to process circumstances.

As a result of my having to process events, sometimes I don't make such a good first impression. One way to counteract that problem is just to always be yourself. If we are authentic, and people see us as the same person all of the time, then second, third, and fourth impressions begin to become reality.

So it is with our witness to our children regarding our faith. As a Christian I believe that the first glimpse of Christ our children should see is when they look upon the face of their parents. But it is really the impression our children get about our faith journey over the long haul that will make a difference in their life.

Perhaps we should meditate on the extent to which our witness to our children, with regard to our personal faith, is authentic, and is consistent day, after day, after day.

⊕

The Locker Room

Guys like to pick. Just ask any man who plays golf and you will hear story after story of the hard times and grief involved in the give and take of men on a golf course. Locker rooms of any kind are merciless when guys go after each other in a no-holds barred verbal dual. Men also know how important it is that they teach their sons how to respond appropriately when they are faced with their first experience of being picked on. There is a fine line between swinging a fist and swinging a piercing comment. These lessons do not come easily. Unfortunately, some boys and men are easy targets. Perhaps they are disabled, or nerdy, or obnoxious, or just "out of it" to the degree that they cannot hold their own. When this is the case, too often there is a "blood in the water" reaction, and these poor people end up as outcasts to be avoided.

I have often wondered if Jesus and his disciples "picked" at one another in a good-natured way. My guess is they did. But Jesus also taught us to love the unlovable by making a decision to love. Jesus decided to love the leper and the blind. Jesus decided to elevate the status of women above that of property. And Jesus decided to love his friends when they abandoned and denied him.

A lady in our community died the other day. She died alone, largely because she was hard to get along with. Her body was found by one of our church members who had made a decision to care for this person who was difficult to care for. Those kinds of decisions to love are what Christ calls us to do.

Let's take some time today to consider someone that we should "decide" to love.

⊕

The Tackle With a Fever

Last Saturday morning, we went to see our grandson play recreation football. He is very young and very big. His position is a down-offensive lineman. We watched the game and I was really disappointed. He was terrible. He would not hit anyone or run until the end of the play. He looked like he was in a fog the entire time. Well, I thought, he should be playing a much better game than this. By 9 p.m. the same day, he was in the emergency room with a high fever. It turned out that he had an ear infection the entire time. If I had known the full circumstances of the situation, instead of thinking that he had had a horrible game, I would have been proud of him for playing his best when he was really sick and probably should not have been on the field at all.

How often do we make judgments regarding others without having a real handle on what their true situation is? I should have known something was wrong with my grandson, because I know him, and what kind of person he is. I should not have assumed the worst. I should have given him the benefit of the doubt.

God gives us the benefit of the doubt, even though He knows all of our circumstances. He loves us when we are at our worst. I believe God honors what is in our hearts, and we know if our hearts are pure.

Perhaps we should spend some time thinking about who we may be judging too harshly, when, if we knew their complete circumstances, our opinion of them might change dramatically.

✠

When Not To Sell Short

My father used to tell me, "Never sell yourself short." Perhaps we should constantly tell ourselves, "Never sell Jesus short." I am often too content to have the easy, comfortable Jesus as my friend. Seldom do I call on the majestic, and powerful, and divine Jesus to walk with me as I deal with the day-to-day issues that are dealt (like a hand of playing cards) to me and each of us every day. We try to play that hand by ourselves, often aware of Jesus' loving presence in our lives, but failing to call on His power in those times of uncertainty and fear. Sometimes I think that I am wary of calling on the power of Christ through the Holy Spirit because I am afraid that I might be too deeply affected by the intensity of a journey with Christ into spiritual depths beyond my comfort zone. Perhaps I am afraid that experiencing the spiritual power of Christ might change me in some fundamental way that I might not like.

A close friend of ours said that she dreaded the day that her husband went off to a spiritual retreat because she liked her old husband just fine, and was afraid of how her husband would be changed if he had a truly powerful spiritual turn around in his life. Guess what? He *did* have that encounter with Christ, and he *did* change as a person in many fundamental ways! The good news is that he was a better husband and dad, and our friend's marriage became even stronger.

We really should consider what it is about ourselves that keeps us from calling on the power of God's Holy Spirit in our lives.

☩

Never Hug a Belly Dancer

Last evening was Anna Lee's birthday. Our youngest adult daughter, Angie, wanted to take her mom to a local Mediterranean restaurant so that we could all watch the belly dancing as we ate. The hidden agenda here was that our granddaughter, Carson, likes to get out on the dance floor and belly dance with the dancer. The dancer was a nice, young, blonde, attractive lady. She entertained us well as she danced with a sword on her head and with flames in her hand. She gyrated and cavorted with us all, and was especially gracious to our little granddaughter, as she often let her leave the table and join her in her "belly" dancing.

On the way out of the restaurant, I gave the young lady a generous tip. As she took the money, she turned to give me a hug. I admit, I was kind of looking forward to it. After all, she was young and pretty, and blonde, and she had few clothes on. Go figure.

Well, as we hugged each other, I learned something else about my new, young female friend. She was also sweaty! After all, she had been dancing all night long. The eagerly anticipated hug had not lived up to my expectations.

So often being disappointed is the result of our expectations when we base them on worldly standards. It does not make any difference if we are looking forward to a new house, or new car, or a new woman. Inevitably, they fail to meet our expectations.

The expectations of our world, when seen through God's eyes, rarely disappoint. When we reflect on those things that God would have us yearn for—peace, patience, love, healthy relationships, and most of all, a relationship with Him, we are never disappointed when we have obtained what He desires us to have.

We should spend some time thinking about how many times in the past that the acquisition of possessions has not lived up to our expectations, and what we could have done and should do differently in the future. With all of that said, I still think about the local Belly Dancer every once in a while. Maybe next time, I'll tip her earlier in the evening!

There's a Mouse in the House

$\mathbf{A}$ close friend of mine was coming to our house the other night. Before he arrived, his wife called and demanded that he call her as soon as her husband arrived. He called her, and on the phone, we all knew that she was "going off on him." It turns out that she thought she had seen a mouse in their house, and she was deathly afraid of mice, and somehow, in her mind, she blamed him for something that she thought she had seen. The problem was not her fear, or even her concern, it was her anger. First of all, he was embarrassed because he had to listen to her rail at him while he was on the telephone at someone else's house. Secondly, their children were there in the house at that time. They heard their mother yelling and screaming at their dad. The children are not stupid. They knew something was wrong. Finally, this anger, expressed so openly and hatefully, produced just a little crack in their relationship. Even if all was forgotten and forgiven in just a few days, even if the couple laughed about the incident weeks later over dinner with friends, this unbridled anger demonstrated that for a very few minutes, one partner disrespected the other to a degree that they verbally abused them.

Men are as just as guilty as women when it comes to the anger issue. Just go to a youth athletic event, or watch a guy react when he thinks he has "caught" someone doing something they should not, or something they deem "stupid." We can all get angry, and almost always that anger does much more harm than good. The consequences of anger are damaged relationships.

Relationships are like fine china, once chipped, even just a little bit, they are still usable and useful, but they are never as beautiful as they were when they were completely whole. It would do us good to reflect on our own anger and its consequences.

✠

Hell Is Overrated

Today I watched a pro football game. It was not particularly well played, and it ended up in overtime. Eventually, one of the teams kicked a field goal and won in sudden death.

It occurred to me that we play many overtime games in our lifetime. OK, you may be thinking, here comes the sales pitch we often hear in the church, "do the right thing, develop a relationship with God, because you might go to bed tonight and not wake up and end up in hell." Could it be that hell is overrated? I don't know for sure, and neither does anyone else. What is important is that failing to develop a spiritual relationship robs us of having the quality of life that God would have for each of us. We do encounter overtimes in life. We are given second chances, not necessarily to "Get right with God" as much as just "To *Get* with God." If we do die tonight, without having developed a spiritual life, the tragedy is that we will have missed out on an entire dimension of our life that could have helped us reach our complete potential as human beings.

By missing out on spirituality, we miss on healing broken relationships and developing healthy ones. By missing out on spirituality, we miss experiencing authentic joy, and so much of the bounty that a relationship with God brings. We are given overtimes in life, and missing out on a relationship with God is a lot worse than missing a winning field goal. Today may be a good time to meditate on the cost of missed opportunities.

☩

Playing Ping Pong With The Devil

When we were raising our children, we had a ping pong table set up in the garage. My wife and I liked to play, and our son became pretty good at the game also. He is now grown and has a house and family of his own. He also has a ping pong table.

Not long ago, we were up at his house at a birthday party for our granddaughter, and several of his friends decided to play ping pong. I was invited along and played the first game. I won, but I was dying inside because I am so out of shape. Then we played another game. I won again, and I am still completely winded. But did I tell anyone? No! I just bragged a little and ragged the guys about letting the old man beat them, but I was not about to play again. I dropped the paddle on the table, made some smart remark, went into another room and collapsed. But I really felt good about winning because I am extremely competitive.

Competition is good. I believe parents should encourage their children to compete and allow them to lose. The experience will be helpful in the long run. It is not too sophisticated anymore to talk about the competition for our souls between the forces of good and evil, but if we are honest with ourselves, we realize that our souls are up for grabs every day. The forces of evil try to convince us that our ego needs to be stroked, and all of our needs need to be met, even at the expense of others. The forces of good move us closer toward submitting to the will of God in our lives. That submission pushes us closer and closer to seeing the good in others and seeking the good for ourselves.

As we go about our days, let us recognize how these opposing forces are playing ping pong for our souls.

☩

Cracking Up The Thermostat

We are redoing our smaller bathroom. Actually, we live in a small 50's style brick ranch with two bathrooms that are not attached to any bedroom. We have named them the girl's bathroom (my wife's), and the boy's bathroom (mine). The boy's bathroom is the one we are fixing up. Anyway, the other night we purchased a new vanity and top that is to be installed in the morning. For a week this vanity has been sitting in its box in our small hall that runs the length of the house. In order to pass by the box and continue up the hall, we have to slide sideways and work our way around it. The big problem is that the thermostat is sitting on the wall opposite, about shoulder high. Every time we pass by the box we bang the thermostat with our shoulder, or head, or elbow, or some other part of our body.

Think about it for a minute. The thermostat is much more important to the operation of the house, but we risked damaging it by leaving the box in the middle of the hall and trying to ease by it without hurting anything. What an analogy for the way we deal with so many of the problems in our lives. Maybe we are having money problems and we try to ease by them and end up damaging our relationship with others and our long term financial well being. Maybe we are unhappy with our jobs, or we drink too much, or are obsessed with porn or gambling, and we try to ease by the problem and end up messing up the most important things in our lives.

How about we move the box? Get it out of the hall, put it out of sight so we don't even think about it, and if we are lucky, we will move it before we break the thermostat.

What are the boxes in our lives that we need to move out of the hall?

☦

The Back of My Pickup Truck

We live in a rather large community (around 125,000), not to have any form of centralized media. We get our newspaper from a neighboring town, and we only have one small a.m. radio station that is hard to find and has the range of a well made kite on a windy day. When politicians run for office here, they print hundreds of signs that wind up in many front yards and by the side of the roads all over town. To get a little broader coverage, magnetic signs go on car doors, and many pickup trucks drive around town with signs in their beds asking for votes for various individuals. I have driven a pickup like this with my own name on a large sign in the back. I will be the first to tell you, my behavior changes dramatically for the better when I know that everyone else knows who I am, and that I am driving the truck. I have better traffic manners, I smile more, I keep the radio down, and generally, try to be a nicer person.

Our faith gives us the opportunity to behave in a transparent way, not because we are afraid that God will "get" us if we don't, but we believe that God knows who we are and we know we are cared for and we want to care back. It is not rocket science. God knows us, we know God, as best we can, and consequently we want to be the best persons we can be—with or without the sign in the back of the pickup.

Let us each be honest about how we behave when only God sees our actions, and what it is that keeps us locked into behavior that makes us unhappy and keeps us small as persons.

Christopher and the Condom Machine

Our grandson, Christopher, is four-years old. A short while ago, we were entertaining some friends from Jamaica, who have a son about Christopher's age. These two guys ran wide open the entire time. One day we decided to take a day trip. We all piled into a big SUV and started off. About ten-miles after we cleared the last town and were well out in the country, both boys decided simultaneously that they had to go to the bathroom. We finally found an old run down gas station. Inside the gas station was some oriental guy frying chicken and potatoes. He immediately told us that he had no restrooms. I was furious because I knew he had to have a restroom on the premises. Maybe he didn't like black and white kids playing together, maybe he was busy, maybe he had his mistress hidden in the bathroom. I didn't know and did not care. I knew we were being treated unfairly. I marched the kids outside, took them to the end of the parking lot, and had them empty their bladders there. Once they were in the car, I went back inside and gave the guy a piece of my mind. I'm sure it made no difference to him. He went on frying his chicken. Then ten-miles up the road, Christopher decides he has to go poop. So I stopped at another gas station and took him inside and found a decent toilet. As he was sitting his tiny bottom on the commode, he looked up, innocently, and saw a condom vending machine on the wall. "What's that Granddaddy?" he asked. I thought and then said lamely, "They sell things that keep men from getting sick, but little boys don't need them." With his eyes saucer-size, Christopher replied, "This sure is some kind of different world over here, isn't it Granddaddy?"

Do we ever get so overcome by events that it seems like we are living in a different world? We probably are living in a world different from that in which God would have us live. Is the world in which we feel most comfortable that same world that God would have for us? It is food for thought, just not fried chicken and potatoes.

⊕

Who Needs a GPS?

We just got a new GPS system for our car. It was a gift from Brian and JJ, our son and daughter-in-law. Brian uses one in his work all the time. He travels and claims he just could not do without his. The one warning he gave us was that we must keep our car locked because these GPS devices are hot items and are popular with those prone to break into cars. Our son-in-law and daughter, Perkins and Christy, just had their house broken into and had a big screen TV stolen from them. They had bought the TV the day before, and evidently, someone followed them home and came back the next day. Now I have to be conscious of locking the car door, and my daughter and her husband are having a home security system put into their house next week. We have to be more careful because we have more stuff.

Think about the relationship between security and possessions. The more possessions we have, the more insecure we become. This view of our world is not the view God would have us see. God would have us find our security in our relationship with Him and others we love. Perhaps we should inventory our possessions and see which of those bring us comfort and security.

⊕

Who Hates Butterflies?

Anna Lee loves butterflies. (Do you ever wonder if there is anyone who hates butterflies?) Anyway, one day recently, I told her that I had seen a butterfly flying near her butterfly house in the front yard. I thought that would be the end of the conversation, but as usual, she wanted more information. "What color was it?" she asked. Now I thought I was doing well just to notice the butterfly. I could have answered, "I don't know what color it was." Or I could have said, "I don't care what color it was." But I did say, cleverly, "It was flying too fast for me to tell." That seemed to satisfy her.

Sometimes I am a genius. But one thing that is clear is that we all spend too much time flying so fast that people cannot tell much about us. And it is true that others fly around so fast that we often cannot tell much about them. But the tragedy is when we fly around so fast that we cannot tell who we really are. In other words, we don't know ourselves. Honestly knowing ourselves is the key to happiness. Hiding our true identity from ourselves leads us down roads that are long, dark, and troubling. How do we come to the point, when we slow down enough to be honest with ourselves, about *who* and *whose* we are? How could we slow down, and if we did, would we get to know ourselves any better?

✝

Winning Is Everything

A couple of years ago, a friend's son began playing in a basketball league where no score was kept. They explained that the kids were taught the fundamentals of the game, and that every player was allowed to try out certain aspects of basketball, such as bringing the ball up the court, and in bounding the ball after a turnover. The players guarded only one player on the other team, and that player was one of equal ability.

"How stupid," I thought. It seemed to me that in real life a score was kept, and that the sooner young people began to experience competition, the better off we all would be. That logic made so much sense back then. Only now, two years later, when my own grandsons are playing in the same league, do I realize how stupid I was and how dead wrong was my opinion. When I had personal experience with the league, my point of view was radically altered. My grandsons are learning the fundamentals of the game and are getting to play and enjoy themselves each and every time they go to the gym.

How true it is that our personal experiences shape our vision. What about our personal experiences with God? We can make judgments about spirituality, but until we have had some experience with that dimension in our lives, our judgments might be just as wrong as mine were about our grandson's basketball experiences. By the way, our oldest, Connor, scored six points in four minutes last Saturday! But who's counting?

Let's reflect for a while on what it is that we are judging without having any real, personal experience with it.

⊕

Cheeseburgers With Ketchup Only

Have you ever heard the saying, "pick your battles carefully?" Well I've never been very good at that. When our children were younger, we used to go to fast food joints a lot. We have three children, and by the time I took everyone's order and got to the counter, I was pretty frazzled. Especially irritating was our youngest daughter who always requested a cheeseburger with ketchup only. Let the person preparing this cheeseburger dare to put a pickle or, God forbid, drop an ounce of mayo on this delicacy, and all heck would break loose. If the order was not perfect, and it often isn't, I would scream at my daughter for being so picky and then take the burger back to the counter and scream at the attendant for being so stupid as to get the order wrong.

As I look back on that time, I am embarrassed. My behavior started to change when two things happened. First, our oldest daughter went to work in a restaurant, and my relationship with God and my spiritual life became a little deeper. The controversy just wasn't worth the effort. I was being a bad dad, a poor citizen, and a hypocrite, all over a stupid cheeseburger!

There are some issues that are so critical that they are worth fighting over, but a cheeseburger with ketchup only, certainly is not one them.

What issues in our life are really inconsequential and evoke unnecessary emotion and conflict?

⊕

Leaving a Tip for God

Another restaurant related issue, about which my views have changed over the years, is tipping. Last week, much of our family went out to a local restaurant. As usually is the case, my wife and I paid for our meal and the meals of our grandchildren. Our adult children were on their own. What a mess! The children were playing with the syrup on the table, moving around from seat to seat, and were generally poorly behaved. We changed our orders a half dozen times, had separate checks—you know the drill. My portion of the tab was $50.00. The same female server (I am trying to be politically correct and not call her a waitress) that waited on our table, checked us out. I tipped her $25.00. She was genuinely surprised and pleased.

Now why do I tell this story? A good friend of mine said that a man of God is a generous tipper because God calls upon us to take care of the poor and widows (single mothers today). The wait staff at restaurants often represent the working poor, and in my mind, deserve our generosity. The most tragic part of this story is that I teach many young adults who work in the food service industry. They have told me for years that the worst time for tipping is on Sundays after church. A lot of those who profess to be the faithful just don't get it.

I believe it would do me good to reflect on those areas of my life where maybe I am just "not getting it." Being honest with ourselves about ourselves is the most important step in becoming that fully human person that God would have us to be.

☩

Killing the Elephant

We went to a beautiful wedding the other evening. The church was wonderfully decorated by the bride's sister who has a real gift for using her creative skills. She did a great job with the flowers and candles. There was a string quartet and a 100 year old organ. The music was outstanding and worshipful. The minister carried off the ceremony to perfection, and the groom and all of the wedding party were dressed to the nines. Everything was perfect.

As the dad walked his gorgeous daughter down the aisle, to my discredit, I could not help but reflect on the fact that he and his wife were presently separated. Their relationship was on the rocks, and to date, we still do not know if they will reconcile.

Our most painful family experiences have a way of raising their ugly heads at family events. I believe, to most of the guests at the wedding, the problems of the mom and dad distracted them to some degree from the celebration of this holy sacrament. The personal problems of the parents were the "elephant in the room." I wondered if the elephant would always be there.

As we reflect on our lives and actions, it may be important to remember that we really don't want to create any elephants in the room. Our decisions, both the good ones and the bad ones, live a life of their own, and they often live to a very old age. We all need the redemption and forgiveness that the Grace of God provides. However, the better approach is to make the good decision the first time around. It doesn't hurt to ask God to show us when we are about to create an "elephant in the room." Kill the elephant before it gets a chance to grow up and dominate our relationships.

✠

Home Improvements

I walk almost every day. Our neighborhood is old and most of the homes are fifties and sixties brick, ranch styles. One particular house that I pass every day really interests me. I knew the original owners, only because I worked for years with their daughter-in-law. I knew the house because it was a showplace in the neighborhood. The owner added a large brick wall around part of the house. He built rock gardens, and stone steps, and was quiet the landscaper. There is even a large greenhouse on the property. The original owner is dead now, and his son and daughter-in-law have moved into the house. But they have not kept it the same. Their improvements are of a different nature. The greenhouse is now used as a studio. The large brick wall and stonework have been replaced by a new garage and playroom.

The point is, I guess, that every generation gets so worked up sometimes about changing things, and redecorating, and having just the right furniture and accessories so everything can be just so, and none of that matters very much. It is easy for us to understand that it is only the content of our hearts and the way we treat others that are really eternal. Easy, that is, until we decide to build that new swimming pool, or add on that room, or change the carpet. It is not that we should not improve and repair and keep up our homes. The problem that so many of us have is that we allow this infatuation with making things over, to substitute for our dealing with the very real issues of repairing and improving our relationships with those in our lives.

Fifty years from now, when someone has purchased the home you are living in now, rest assured the carpet will be changed out again and the color scheme will be different. Fifty years from now, if we have maintained our relationships and taken care of those we love and those that God puts in our path, there will be no need for renovation.

What is it in our lives that we need to be sure to maintain?

✠

Size Doesn't Matter

There are tons and tons of mega churches, of all descriptions, springing up all around us. These churches have huge multimedia budgets, rock bands, handsome ministers, and wonderful programs for members of all ages. They market themselves like crazy, and literally thousands of worshipers show up on Saturday night and Sunday morning and leave, telling everyone they know how wonderful their huge Church is. That is not a bad thing if those churches are helping others foster their relationship with God in an authentic way.

On the other hand, we talked to a young man last week who was telling us about the small, rural church in which he grew up. The church was located in the corn belt in the Midwest. It was small with few programs, especially for the children and youth. The church did not have services every Sunday, and often did not have a permanent minister. Despite all of the apparent shortcomings of his little home church, he said, in summary, "You know, we didn't have much, but we got love right."

What a cool and insightful message this young man had. He "got" it. In our families, churches, neighborhoods, and even our work places, neither sparkle, or size, or perception, or material goods, matter very much. What matters most is do we "get love right." When we take the time to examine ourselves, our organizations, and most importantly, our relationships, whether we "get love right" makes all of the difference.

☦

Our Nasty Carpet

What an interesting week this has been. Our carpet in our bedroom was nasty. When we bought this house, four or five years ago, our bedroom had a white, fluffy carpet, which was kind of dirty then, and now is intolerable. We pulled up the carpet and have been refurbishing the hardwood floors underneath. Our bedroom furniture was spread out all through the house. About that time the dryer went out. Then the disposal started to leak. Everything seemed to be going wrong at the same time. If all of this had happened even ten years ago, I might have overreacted and been upset and frustrated. I probably would have screamed, cursed, wailed and moaned. I might have looked for someone to blame.

Years ago, Anna Lee and I would probably have ended up fussing with each other in the midst of all of the confusion and calamity. Now it's different. Not that we handle unexpected problems perfectly, but I think we both have figured out not to become too upset over things we cannot control, and to also understand that "things" like carpet and disposals are not nearly as important as we once thought they were.

If there is a life-lesson here, it may be that taking things in stride requires that we develop a perspective in life that helps us understand that we should not put too much stock in the transient—those things that are not going to last. That perspective also helps us understand what we can and cannot control. When someone says, "don't sweat the small stuff", they make it seem too easy. Not sweating the small stuff, the transient issues in our lives, is difficult. It takes prayer and meditation to sort out the small stuff from the important stuff. We will never get all the way there. Maybe some small stuff we should sweat after all. That's why we fixed the dryer first. Anna Lee said so.

How much time do we spend emotionally involved with things we cannot control or that don't really matter very much?

Time Passes

Compound interest has been called the ninth wonder of the world. One aspect of our lives that identifies the passage from boyhood into manhood, should be the realization that time passes. For many of us, though, we have not really figured that out. Take me, for instance. If I eat a cheeseburger at 12 noon and go to the scales and weigh at 12:15, I am very likely to weigh the same as I did at 11:45. Weigh again at 8 am the next day and, well…time passes. Just go buy a car with no payments for 90 days. What does the banker know that we have not figured out? "Time Passes." On a more positive note, put up a couple of hundred dollars a month into savings or the market when you are 21 years old, and when you are 51, you truly get the message when you get your bank statement—time passes. Don't service your car—time passes, don't paint your house, or change your air conditioner filters— well, you get the idea.

Another aspect of this truth of life is that time passing is a terribly important concept when it comes to our relationships. Don't respect your wife—time passes. Don't spend time with your children, or anyone you love, and suddenly there is conflict or crises, and you get the phone call late at night that circumstances have changed and we will never get the opportunity to make up that lost time. Isn't it ironic that when someone dies we say that they have "passed away?" How about our spiritual lives? Put off prayer, meditation, worship, humility and sacrifice, and before we know it, we have drifted so far away from our own spirituality that we are in danger of not recognizing how God can work and has worked in our lives.

Let us think a little bit about what part of our lives, be they physical, spiritual, or relational, that we have let time get the best of. Also, we don't need to buy anything with no payment for 90 days. Time passes.

⊕

All In The Family

Today, several of our family members went back to a small community where we had lived almost 30 years ago. The little church there was having a "homecoming" service, and we were invited to come back for the service and dinner afterwards. Although we have seen a few of the people from the town over the years, essentially today was like going back three decades in a time machine. We had had very good and very difficult experiences in this community. We were young and made the mistakes of youth, and were nurtured by wonderful, older people. We honed many of our skills there. Skills that later led to some professional, personal, and relational successes. The town was and is so small that there are only 600 people in the city limits. Our little church had about 100 people show up on Sunday morning.

What I felt today was overwhelming. Many of the older members of the community had died and, of course, we have all gotten older. But the shared love each person there felt for one another was both humbling and exciting in a very special way.

On the way out of town, we drove the route that I used to run each night when I jogged after a long day at work. We stopped by our old house, and even drove through the cemetery on our way out of town to read the family names on the tombstones. These names, once so familiar, were, in most cases, tributes to lives well lived.

What's the point here? Well, there isn't one especially, except to say that the experience that we had today was a tribute to the relationships that we had fostered so many years ago. These relationships were built on almost unconditional acceptance of one another. For in a town of 600 people, we knew, often in very realistic and graphic terms, not only knew each other's strengths but also each other's weaknesses. Born from that knowledge was a certain vulnerability that made us very "real" to one another. From that firsthand knowledge of who we really were as people, these relationships that have held up over the years were fostered. It might be worthwhile to consider who do we know now, in such a "real" way, that the mutual acceptance and love that we share with one another will still be holding up 30 years down the road.

Pass the Remote

I have a terrible time focusing on anything. It may be that more men have focusing issues than we have realized. Take the remote control. I simply cannot stand to watch TV without the remote in my hands. I channel surf and move from program to program, check the news and sports scores, all the while theoretically watching one TV show. One of my closest friends keeps his laptop on a little table beside him in his den, and as he watches TV or a movie, researches any thought that comes into his head about the content of his show. My son-in-law's blackberry is always in his hand. He knows everything that is going on all the time. Lucky him. I can't speak for women but the guys I know are very distracted. It bothers me the most on the golf course. I will have two or three good holes, and then my mind starts to wander, and my game starts to tank.

It might be that this distractibility is taking a heavy toll on our spiritual life. How difficult it is to concentrate on God and see God's work in everyone and everything we encounter? Concentrating on God takes more effort than time. We have to consciously decide that we are going about our day looking for and experiencing the living spirit of God present in the world. Maybe we should have little crutches to remind us to look for God. Perhaps every time we open a car door we program our minds to think of God. Every time we turn on the water, or wash our hands, or change the channel on the TV, we pause and concentrate on God's presence.

The ironic thing about continually seeking God out during our day, is that our concentration on things in general improves. We do a better job listening to others, our time management improves, and we actually get more accomplished if we involve God in the process. Concentrating and focusing on God is not a technique for a better life. Focusing on God is our calling. Focusing on God is the central purpose of our lives. Focusing on God is what we were put on this Earth to do. The byproduct is a better life, perhaps even a better golf game!

Let us consider when and how we focus on God each day.

Riding With The Top Down

We have a 15 year old Mustang convertible. Actually, I have a Mustang convertible, and Anna Lee tolerates a Mustang convertible. Two days ago, I began having trouble with the small power window, just behind the driver's seat. I was afraid for a while that I was not going to get the window up. Much to my relief, the window did come up, once I messed with it a little while. I know I will have to have it fixed, but I will spend some time finding the right person to do this job for the right price. In the meantime, I have been riding with the top down, but this little window left up. It looks dorky this way and absolutely destroys the lines of the car. Someone said to me that I surely was not going to ride around with the top down and the window up, and I responded, "why not, I love riding with the top down every chance I get." I don't ride with the top down because I want to show off the car (although I am accused of such by Anna Lee). I don't even ride with the top down because I like the way it feels. I ride with the top down because something deep inside me tells me that I have a basic "top-down" nature; that I am happiest and most content with myself when the top is down.

Excuse me for comparing worshiping God with riding with the top down, but yesterday at the car wash, while I was watching the car being cleaned up, I came to believe there are some similarities. We do not worship God because we want to look good in front of others. We certainly don't worship God because it makes us feel good. We worship God because something in our deepest nature sends us a signal that we have been placed here to worship God, and it is in that worship that we can find great happiness, joy and contentment.

For me, I ride with the top down because that is the natural thing for me to do. If I were to ride in a hard top for years, I might forget that I am a top-down person.

Have we failed to worship God for so long that we have forgotten that we are at our best when we are worshiping Him? Let us spend some time in reflection on the degree to which it is in our nature to worship God.

A Card in the Wastebasket

I just got back from the gym, and my wife, Anna Lee, told me that someone had called. She left the number on the backside of a business card that was lying on our desk. I returned the call, and about two minutes ago, I just hung up the telephone, and I feel really crappy. For several years, I had worked with a guy named Bud, who was about ten years my senior. Bud had moved into our town at an older age than normal and taken a job with our organization in order to build some retirement before it was too late. He was a boisterous fellow, a former football coach who had done a lot of things and had been a lot of places. He was sort of restless. But he did good work and we worked together on the same team for several years until he retired. Bud stayed in town and built a few houses to supplement his retirement. We would run into each other at the grocery store or the golf course. He smoked too much, and had a bout with cancer that he said was in remission. Bud had a son who had also joined our organization, and recently, I saw on our personnel report that the son had moved out of town, so I called my friend, Bud, to see what was up.

After leaving several messages, he just called back a few minutes ago. Bud said that he had sold his house and moved with his son to Kentucky. "I'm 75 now and I don't know how much longer I have," he said. He told me that his wife had wanted to move away with his son's family, fearing that if Bud died, she would be left alone. We talked for a few minutes. He told me about his new situation. He did not seem all that happy, just reconciled to his situation. Bud invited us to come and see him, and he told me one more time that his health was good, and not to worry about him. We hung up saying that maybe we would see each other again someday—each of us knowing that it would very likely never happen.

I wrote Bud's telephone number in my book (the low tech way still works well), and tossed the business card with his number on the back into the waste basket. It seemed so final to watch that card float into the bin.

What does all this mean? Maybe that we should treat others well, value them for their contribution, and realize that none of us "know how much longer we have." Sometimes when others leave us, someone will say to them, "God's Speed." In that God is Love, perhaps God's speed means something like, "You will be missed, we love you because God only made one of you, and we are a little less blessed with you no longer in our lives."

It might be worth reflecting on whom should we tell that to now, before they leave us. By the way, "God's speed, Bud."

Why Women Run Things

If you spend much time in a church, you figure out pretty quickly that it's the women who are running things. The guys may appear to be in charge, but by and large women call the shots. Many guys avoid Church. They don't verbalize much about the spiritual aspects of their lives, and they think if they go to church they will be made to feel uncomfortable and probably asked to talk about things that they consider private. But underneath their dismissive attitude, men really think a great deal about the ultimate purpose of their lives, and often, when probed, their observations are stoically perceptive. It may be that men feel that churches and most religions want to snuggle up to God, and most guys don't want to snuggle, they want to get to the point. Guys might also think that if they become too "religious" it will make it hard to go out with the guys and grab a beer and cruise good looking women and tell locker room jokes.

The trick is for organized religion to figure out that God is a lot more about the "do's" than the "don'ts". If there was ever a person of action, it was Jesus. He fed the hungry, He healed the sick, and He took on the established church in such an *in your face* manner, that it eventually got him killed. Hanging on a cross and asking God, "Where the hell are you?" is not exactly snuggling up to religion.

The scriptures are filled to the brim with Men's Men. David had his lover's husband killed and paid a dear price for it. Solomon threatened to cut a baby in half for Goodness sake; and

Peter cut the ear off a guy when he threatened Jesus. There is a catch, however, regarding this testosterone thing. All of these men had an incredibly close relationship with God. It did not make them any less masculine, but their relationship with God changed their lives profoundly. I think Peter still checked out the good looking women that he saw on the dusty, middle eastern roads, and David probably still had a glass of wine with the guys after a hard day of being king. But both of these "men's men" knew that God was at work in their lives in profound ways. They had experienced God and they worked hard to maintain that relationship. They put their fear of looking too religious behind them. They became men of God, and that decision required more testosterone than any other.

What is it about being a man that helps or hurts our relationship with God?

⨁

Don't Do Anything Stupid

Last week I had an appointment with my cardiologist. I was not feeling all that well, and was not looking forward to my appointment. She didn't like the way my heart was beating and fixed me up with a heart monitor for 24 hours. In that 24 hour period, I played golf, got sued, and had my laptop stolen! (Not necessarily in that order.) When I told her what had happened during that time period, she was not impressed. My heart rate was much too slow. She was worried and decided to change my medication around. Now the real message of this story is that I had already changed my medication around on my own without asking her, and had completely screwed up the way my heart beats to the point that it could have been a very bad scene. She straightened me out in short order.

How many times do we, who are sick morally or personally, try to straighten out our messes on our own and screw things up even more? In many ways, our relationship with God is like our relationship with our physicians (who was the great physician again?). We are sick to start with, we ask for help and guidance, it is given, and then we either do not follow the instructions, or do like I did and try to improve on the instructions that were given, because we think we know a little bit more about our current condition than God does. I don't like trite phraseology like, " Let go and let God", as if we just get into a sail boat and let God push us around the ocean of life and we live happily ever after. It doesn't work like that. We are screwed up in one way or another from the get go. God is there, not to just to sweep us off our feet, but there to keep us on our feet. God's prescription for our lives is more about giving us broad guidelines (love God, love others, and don't do anything stupid). Those guidelines bring balance, responsibility, and satisfaction with the way our lives are going.

It may be worthwhile to reflect on how we are adjusting our own medication, and changing the guidelines that God has given us, and that serve us so well.

☩

Life Comes At You Fast

There is a commercial out there that says, "Life comes at you fast..." And it does. What are our kids going to do the first time someone offers them pot or propositions them to have sex? We can teach our children about the ill effects of casual drug use. We can fill our children's heads full of the latest statistics about sexually transmitted diseases or unwanted pregnancy. We know, though, that information alone will do little good when the joint is being passed around the car, headed for your child, or two hormone-filled adolescents find themselves "home alone." We need to help our children plan ahead for the situation so they do not get caught up in the moment.

Planning ahead is everything. Last week an organization, with which I am deeply involved, hosted a major event. It did not go well. Although I was not directly involved in planning the event, ultimately I bore a good deal of responsibility for the performance of those responsible in directing the activities. This week I have been answering several angry emails the old fashioned way-by telephone. My message is, yes, the event did not go as smoothly as we had hoped, and yes, we are already taking corrective measures to ensure this does not happen again. Lame—right? I could have just said, "We are locking the barn door after the horse has gotten out." We do not want either ourselves or our children to be worried about open barn doors.

By not planning ahead, we do leave the barn door open with our relationships with others and also with God. How many times have we said or acted toward others in a way that we have regretted? It could be that we have not planned ahead from a relational perspective. That really is what having a spiritual foundation, with God working in our lives, allows us to do. We are planning ahead, so that when that moment of crisis, or anger, or disappointment, or important decision making comes, we are guided by God's Spirit, and God has "planned ahead" for us, and we end up doing the right thing.. As a result, we less often hurt others or ourselves, or ignore opportunities to offer the "peace" that God provides to those around us. Having God's Spirit within us gives us the opportunity to look down the long road so when that bump or curve comes at us we have already planned on how we are going to react. After all, life comes at you fast.

How are we coming at planning ahead with regard to our relationships?

☩

Who We Really Are

Today our niece, Suzanne, is having very serious surgery. She has been battling breast cancer for some time, and her prospects are good, even though this surgery is serious. Her husband, our nephew, sends out regular emails updating their many friends and family on her condition. It is amazing how encouraging his emails are to those that receive them. Our nephew's name is John. John is bright and focused, and he is into all kinds of "guy" stuff. He plays a mean hand of poker, holds season tickets to his favorite NFL team, can make or fix almost anything, and basically built his own house. But these emails have shown a side of John that helps us understand that he and Suzanne are persons with a deep spiritual life that has a certain clarity and realism to it that is a blessing to others. It seems to me while we are reading these emails that their power lies in his making himself authentic and vulnerable without whining and wallowing in self pity, even though many would say that after all that he and Suzanne have gone through, they might be due a pity party. As I write this, Suzanne, our niece, and John, her husband, are courageously facing one of the many difficult days that have been and will continue to be part of their journey together. By being real about their struggles and their triumphs they have been a powerful witness to so many others that they know and love.

Their transparency makes me wonder how much more our lives could affect others in powerfully positive ways if we were to be as real and vulnerable as our niece and nephew, John and Suzanne. Right now all we can do is to pray for them, to let them know how proud of them we are, and try to emulate the very meaningful way that they are sharing their faith with others.

How honest are we with others about the issues we are facing?

☦

Who Is Sending Me To Hell?

Once we buy into believing in God, there is a stark realization that most of the universal questions and concepts that men have asked or thought about over the years have to go unanswered and unproven by fact. One of these concepts that we will never understand is hell. Is there one, what is it like, and how can a God whose self definition is "Love" allow for a place like hell in the universe? I do know a little bit about Hell though. What I know was taught to me by an old, black man named George Weston that I met many years ago. I was young, inexperienced, and stupid, and I went to work with a small organization, and within a couple of years, I pretty much found myself as the man in charge. Looking back now, with 30 plus more years of experience, I realize now that I really didn't know one of my orifices from a hole in the ground (you can figure that out and it might still be the case)! Anyway, we had a guy working for us that was a real pain in the same place.

One day George was in my office and I was complaining about the other man's pettiness. George looked at me and smiled and said, "You know, I don't think I would let another person send me to hell." I've thought about the wisdom in that remark so much over my life, especially lately.

We have two neighbors, both named Sam, and both over 80 years old. The first Sam is alone and needs some help with his yard and housekeeping. The second Sam refuses to acknowledge that there is any problem at all and discourages anyone that wants to go help Sam #1. Why do you ask, would Sam #2 have so much contempt for Sam #1? The answer lies in some minor dispute that goes back to the 1960's. The sadness in this decades old dispute is that Sam #2 is allowing something Sam #1 did to offend him years ago, send him to hell. He is letting another's actions fill his life with a sorriness of attitude that is taking a portion of joy from his own life. Life indeed is too short and too complicated and too important to let one person's behavior rob another person of its joy. We don't need to let another person send us to the hell of a joyless life. Thank you, George Weston… Are we letting the fact that we are upset with another person send us to hell?

I Want a Bobcat

For two or three years, Anna Lee, and I went down to the Mississippi coast to help out in the aftermath of Katrina. The devastation was unbelievable, and in the beginning we were busy volunteers mucking out houses and cleaning up what seemed to be an endless supply of limbs and litter that saturated miles and miles of the Mississippi Coast. After a while, the "grunt" work was mostly done, and the volunteers began to become more skilled-carpenters, plumbers, electricians and the like. We were pretty much left to cooking for the group and cleaning up the camp as the more skilled workers plied their trades. There was one man there that did interest me. He was from Kansas, I think, and he had a bobcat with a front end loader on one end. He would leave his bobcat parked on the side of the road when he went back home, but regularly he showed up and started his "toy", as he called it, and off to work he would go. He said that this was his mission and his contribution on the Gulf coast was enormous over the years that he came.

I really envied that guy. He seemed so sure of what he believed God was calling him to do and so capable as he did it. Just last month, many years removed from our work in Mississippi, I was cutting the grass of one of our neighbors who has fallen on hard times. I was a little worried that my mower might get torn up, and I was a little frustrated that there were old bricks and limbs in the yard, that I was constantly dodging or stopping to pick up. It did dawn on me eventually that my little lawnmower was kind of like the bobcat that guy from Kansas had. My lawnmower was not as cool and sexy as the bobcat, but I was doing the best I could with what I had to work with.

There is some comfort in knowing that you are doing the best you can at the time. I wonder how many of us don't do enough because we have yet to figure out that it is OK to work with what we have at the moment. It is different for all of us. Some of us may have tools, others may just have time to spend online or on the phone lending a hand to someone who needs it. For me, the best I had that day was my little riding lawnmower, and that was enough to get the job done. It would be cool, though, to have one of those bobcats.

What tools do we have ready right now that we can put to use for others?

Fixing the Weed Eater

If any of you guys out there want to make a ton of money, you need to come to our hometown and open a small engine repair shop. For some reason or the other, even though we are a fairly good sized city, we only have one real place to go have your lawnmowers, chain saws, and other small engine tools repaired. These people would qualify as the small engine Nazis! They act like they are God's gift to anyone who has a problem that they may or may not fix, depending on their mood for the day. I went down to their shop not long ago to pick up a weed eater that I had left a long, long time before. Basically they said it was not worth fixing and charged me $15.00 for looking at it. That would not have been so bad except they were so arrogant in their attitude. I had to wait a few minutes for them to tell me they did not have a part I wanted for another piece of equipment. While I waited, I decided to see if anyone in the shop smiled or laughed at anything. No such luck. Two or three other guys came in and they were treated rudely and nobody ever had anything but a sorry, grumpy look on their faces. When the fellow came to give me the news that he could not find the part I needed, I intentionally smiled back at him and tried to make some type of lame joke. Still no reaction. I left the building really feeling sorry for the people inside. There appeared to be absolutely no joy in their lives at all.

This may be a really judgmental statement, but I bet we all know others who have no joy in their lives. God wants us to be joyous, even in the face of tough times, but especially when we are going about our daily routines and have the opportunity to touch the lives of others. The joy we find in God's presence in our lives is not a trumped-up attitude. The joy we receive, as we relate to God, comes really from a peace or relaxed view of life that comes from experiencing the pleasure of having God in our lives. That phrase, "Having God in our lives", has been used so much in such a casual manner that it has become trivialized and meaningless. That is so unfortunate because having God in our lives can make all the difference in the way we view ourselves and those around us. Those with God in their lives are certainly not perfect and do not have perfect lives. But they sure beat the heck out of the joyless lives those guys down at the lawnmower shop seem to have bought into! And furthermore, my weed eater still is not working!

It may do us good to consider the degree to which we have joy in our own lives.

⊕

The Rat and the Tower

Tucked into the center of Western North Carolina is a mountain called Pisgah. Pisgah may be the most well known of all of the Western North Carolina mountains, even though it is not the highest (Mt. Mitchell), or even the second highest (Clingmans Dome). Pisgah's notoriety comes from a rat-shaped ridge line that lies at its foot, and an old television tower that extends from its peak. When I was a child growing up in those mountains, I remember the excitement that came with having the tower erected on Pisgah. That tower meant that we were going to have a local television station and that we would be plugged into the world. Years later, when television towers no longer served any useful purpose, someone suggested that the tower be removed from the peak of the mountain. The residents there resisted. They had become used to seeing the tower from miles and miles away. The tower had become part of who they were, part of their neighborhood. The tower had actually become part of what Mt. Pisgah was, and, to them, always would be. Nope, it won't happen. Sometime in the future the tower will be gone. Either a younger generation without the emotional ties to the tower will dismantle it, or gravity will win in the end, as it always does.

When my mother was a little girl, around 1920, her father took her camping at Mt. Pisgah. When she and my father were "courting", they drove their model "T" (or "A", I really can't remember which) Ford up to the base of the mountain and walked to the top. Years later, when my sister and I were young, we took family picnics up to the mountain and spent the afternoon hiking to the top. Our children have spent time on Pisgah, and I imagine that our grand children and their children will also enjoy the mountain.

What's the point? The mountain stays, the tower goes. The mountain is of God, the tower is of man. The mountain is eternal, the tower is temporal.

Last weekend we were up at the Biltmore House in Asheville, NC, with our son and two of our grandchildren. We stepped out on the balcony to take their picture and I could not help but notice Pisgah and the "rat" in the background. I thought of my mother and my dad and of all who have come and gone and will come and go up and down and around that grand old mountain. Then I noticed the TV tower sticking up like a straight pen from the apex of the mountain peak. The tower did not bother me in the least. Let it stay there for a while longer if that makes people happy. It will be down soon enough. The tower is just not here to stay. The mountain, "Pisgah", will be there forever.

Tonight I will try to meditate on the value of the eternal things of God.

✠

Driving a Straight Stick

A really nice, feel good movie came out a while back entitled, *The Bucket List*. The movie basically asked the question, "What things do you want to do before you die?" It is a fair question and I have a few things on my list. I would like to drive into all 48 contiguous states in the USA. I would like to cruise through the Panama Canal. I would like to see my granddaughters happily married, and find out where my great grandfather is buried. I would like to go back to Normandy and silently walk through the cemetery there and thank all of those buried beneath that ground for the freedom that we enjoy. I would like to own, for the first time in 40 years, a straight stick sports car, (not fancy mind you), that makes you feel like you are really driving. I would like to hike Mt. Pisgah (already mentioned) one more time, and go camping in a small tent with my wife, and wake up in the morning and cook eggs and bacon and brew coffee over a camp stove. I also would like to go to the Holy Land and see for myself many of the places I have read about in the scriptures all these years.

This is a short, personal bucket list of some of the things I want to do. The only problem is that we have almost asked the wrong question. A real bucket list should not ask, "what do we want to do before we die." A real bucket list should ask, "what kind of person do we want to become before we die. Do we want to become decisive, or powerful, or respected, or thoughtful, or generous, or delightful? Maybe we want to become more spiritual and compassionate, or accepting, or a person of inner peace who lives abundantly. Who knows what kind of person we want to become, but we need to ask the question.

It may be that through prayer and meditation and personal honesty we can get a clear picture of the kind of person we are, and then seek to become the kind of person that we want to be.

⊕

Frank Sinatra Was a Dope

With apologies to Frank Sinatra, the song, "I Did It My Way", is kind of stupid. We all do it our way, some of our ways are just better than others.

I remember the day my father died. I was at work and received a frantic telephone call from my mother. All she said was, "he's on the floor, he's had a heart attack, the EMTs are working on him." This was before cell phones. I tore out of my office and drove home as fast as I could and called her back. No answer. I threw some clothes in a suitcase and rushed to the airport. That took about an hour. When I got to the airport, I called my mother again. My nephew answered the telephone and confirmed the worst. My father had had a heart attack and was dead before he hit the floor. He was 70 years old. It was almost 25 years ago.

I have been thinking lately about talking to our adult children about how to deal with the "phone call" when they get theirs about their mother or me. What should you tell someone you love about your own death? My children need to know that their dad has few regrets. My children need to know that their dad loves his family more than life itself. My children need to know that the screw ups that life brings us must be there or we would never recognize the good times when they come around. Most importantly, I want my children to know that if we do our best to have a relationship with God, then God honors what is in our hearts. I am absolutely convinced of that. Each of our efforts to build that relationship look different and are unique spiritual journeys. I would like my children to remember that I took my best shot, never really understood God, but learned that if God is God, then God could not be understood. I enjoyed life, I will miss them greatly, but I am excitedly curious about what is yet to come.

It might be profitable to spend some time thinking about what we would want to tell our children about the phone call they will get someday.

⊕

I Doubt It

The real problem with God, for me, is that sometimes my faith runs so strong and I understand completely that if God is God I will never understand Him, and that seems really cool to me. Putting one's faith in a supernatural God is exciting and comforting and really, in an odd sort of way, intellectually stimulating. But every day is not that kind of day. Every so often, I doubt. OOOH! The dreaded "D" word! The doubt creeps in my mind because when I spend a good deal of time focusing on God, my brain tries to take over, and I try to understand the "God" concept that I cannot understand, and then I start to doubt, and I kind of think in my mind, " Man, what if God isn't there after all?" Then what does all of this mean?

One evening I was in a prison with a bunch of guys doing a prison ministry retreat. One of my companions on the retreat said something to the effect that I was a "searcher." To this day I am not sure if he meant that to be a compliment, a criticism, or just an observation. One thing I know is that he was right. For the better part of my adult life, I have searched for God. At times that search has lead to enormous spiritual highs, but the price one pays for searching for God is, that at times, that search leads to honest doubt. Guess what? It's OK. God can deal with it. As a matter of fact, I find it comforting to think that God may take joy in one who searches and maybe even winks his eternal eye when that doubt begins to creep into our minds.

The contemporary author, Wayne Dyer, reminds us that the poet Alfred Lord Tennyson, when describing the doubter, said, "There lives more faith in honest doubt, believe me, than in half the creeds." Tennyson wrote these words in the mid 1800's. Guys have been searching for God, doubting God's existence and nature, and ultimately finding God for a long, long time. I truly believe that God honors this search and the honest doubt that we have. I also truly believe that the only way to experience God is by searching for him.

Perhaps we should spend some time reflecting on how our personal search is going.

Turning Down the Sound

Anna Lee and I were at the gym last week walking the treadmill. We like the gym that we go to. We usually go around 9 p.m. and walk for an hour. Of course, she gets in more mileage than I do. My point of view is that I value a quality walk over a quantity walk, but who cares. The important thing about our treadmill experience is the individual TV imbedded into each machine. With headphones, we can watch whatever we want and not disturb others.

Last week an interesting thing happened. A couple of people using some equipment in the next row over from us left their TV's on when they had finished their workout. We could see those TV screens but not hear any sound. On one station there was a reality show in which a professional athlete was living large. He had women, cars, money, and just about anything one could want. On the other channel, some gangster looking guy was choosing between several women who continually had the "pick me", "pick me", mindset. Even though they were grown women, they acted like they were in junior high. Both shows had kind of a soft porn motif, if that is not an oxymoron. What struck me was not the content of the shows, even though both were cheap and tacky. I could not help but wonder what our lives would look like if someone was watching with the sound off. What impression would we give others about who we are, and what view would others have of the quality of our lives? Really, what we say has very little to do with who we are.

An interesting meditation exercise might be to replay the actions of our day from the point of view of the silent TV screen. A very profound prayer would be to ask God to allow those who are watching our lives unfold, without the sound, to see His presence in our lives.

✛

Rain Checks

It is late Friday morning. In a few minutes I will be going to town to buy a light lunch for my wife, Anna Lee, who is out shopping. I will bring it home and we will enjoy it together. Right now I am sitting at our computer with the house in total silence, except for the sound of a steady rain falling on the trees that surround our little home. Our dogs are curled up on the floor sleeping. Things are very peaceful right now. Earlier today I got up and took a friend's daughter to school. They had had a family emergency and had called the house last night to ask for our help. After that, our regular foursome met at the golf course. We got in four holes before the thunderstorms drove us into the clubhouse. We sat inside for almost an hour, around the table, drinking coffee and watching, out of the corner of our eye, the news playing on the TV mounted on the ceiling. We enjoyed the conversation, but eventually left the golf course behind with rain checks in our pockets, and headed home.

All in all, it has been a wonderful morning. First, in a very small way, our family was able to offer help to someone that needed it. Secondly, I was able to spend time with old friends who really like being in each other's company. Finally, I have been able to spend a good bit of time in silence in kind of thoughtful, meditative, and prayerful moments. These moments have helped me experience the presence of God in the little things that have made up this day so far. This does not happen often, but this morning God's Spirit has brought with it genuine peace and thanksgiving for the wonderful routine of life and the bounty that fine friendships add to our daily journey.

It might be worthwhile to appreciate the routine of our lives and to acknowledge God's presence in all that we do.

☩

Betting On God

It seems that, often in today's world, especially in western culture, people want to be able to prove everything. I remember when I was a kid and someone else would make some comment that was kind of confrontational, we would often respond, "PROVE IT!" That's kind of the way people who do not know God are towards those of us who believe in and have experienced the presence of God—they want us to prove it. That's a trap not to get caught up in. But I do sometimes think that it is not altogether completely illogical to believe in God. Does it not make as much sense that a God would have created the universe as it would to believe that everything we know of was created randomly, by chance?

Last week one of our old friends was released from jail, where he spent a month, and it turns out he was completely exonerated. When he walked into our house, the joy and relief that we felt for him and his family were incredible. We all literally were leaping with joy, and his wife, who lives in another country over a thousand miles away, wept openly on the telephone as the sound of his voice reached her for the first time in months. I have witnessed the overwhelming emotion that military families feel when they see for the first time their loved one coming home from a dangerous overseas deployment. Is it not just as rational to believe that this joy, peace, love, and overwhelming emotion that we, as humans feel, in terms of our relationships to one another, are signs of our own humanity, and are rooted in an eternal God that made us in His own image? I don't try to prove the existence of God. I have learned to take that on faith. But even in a rational world, if I had to bet, I would put my chips on His divine presence in our lives.

Tonight when I go to bed, I am going to meditate about when and how I am aware of God's divine presence in my life.

⊕

A Solar Eclipse

Today is Monday. Yesterday, Anna Lee and I had the distinct privilege of taking communion (The Lord's Supper) to an elderly couple who lives just down the street. They are charter members of our church, and have lived in our neighborhood since 1959. The man, Sam, has Parkinson's disease and the lady, Jean, just returned home from a rehab center where she was recovering from a difficult fall that she took while she was getting her mail. Their last name is Hendry. The Hendry's have a big lot at their house, and from time to time the grass gets out of control. Not long ago I cut their grass for them. That was while Jean was in the hospital and Sam was getting around the house as best he could by himself. Sam is a really thoughtful man. Thoughtful in the sense that he understands what is going on around him and sees beneath the surface on a variety of matters.

Yesterday, as we were leaving, he gave me $20.00. At first I thought that it was his gift to the church's communion fund for the poor that he wanted me to put in the offering for him. But he asked if I had ever heard the story of the man who lived before people understood what was going on during an eclipse of the sun. I told him no and he went on to say that when the sun began to get dark the man got on his horse and went around paying off all of his debts because he thought the world was going to end and he did not know how much time that he had. "I have got some things I want to get done now because the sun is getting dark," he said. "Take this money at least to help pay for the gas you used when you where cutting my gas. I've been meaning to do this for some time now."

I took his money and will take it tomorrow and give it to the communion fund or give it to someone else who needs it. But what I do with that money is beside the point. The point is that I need to determine what things I need to get done now because the sun is getting dark, for I do not know how much time I have left.

How important is it for all of us to consider Sam's story of the man and the eclipse and maybe, if we need to, get on our horses and start taking care of business.

Picking a Winner

We had a pretty good day today from a victory stand-point. All three of our grandchildren's teams won in the games in which they played. Carson, our granddaughter, and Christopher, our grandson, both won their soccer games, and our oldest grand-son, Connor, won his football game. All three of the children did well, but they all should probably study hard and go to college just in case they do not have a pro career. After the games, Christopher and EJ, his younger brother, (you are keeping up with this) and their dad, Perkins, came over to our house to eat lunch and watch college football. This was especially cool because we don't get to see Perkins very often. All of the teams we were pulling for won and he took the two boys home early in the afternoon. The boys reappeared around dinner time. It was our daughter and their mother, Christy's, 40th birthday, and we had the boys sleep over with us while their mom and dad went out for the evening. They were great and went to bed early and we had had a really good day.

When Anna Lee and I went to bed that evening, we were reflecting on a talk, or sermon, or devotion of some kind that we had heard. It suggested that we thank God for the victories in our lives. We really were kind of laughing a little about all of our teams winning when we both began to think of the most important victory of the day. It was Christy's 40th birthday. She has had type-one diabetes since she was 4 years old. At the time, the doctors warned us that after 20 years serious complications would set in. So far she is free of complications and is managing her disease very well. She did not think she would have children, and now she has two wonderful sons. Anna and I quickly realized that we should thank God for this incredible victory in our lives.

I cannot explain the theological issues associated with what I have just written. I know all the questions that arise with giving God the credit for Christy's good health, or that of anyone else. But Anna Lee and I know that we do indeed need to give God thanks for this victory, even though we do not understand it. In a Saturday of victories, having our daughter with us for all these years is the greatest victory of all. Can we spend some time in re-flection on the victories that we have had in our own lives?

Ordinarily Courageous

There are two friends of mine who are just regular guys. They both are professionals at their jobs, and both have kind of regular families. Each has had some struggles with their children, but as their kids are getting older, these problems seem to be working themselves out. Each of my friends has been married to their wives for many years. Some would call their lives boring. I would prefer to think of both of them as courageous. We have breakfast together each week.

Last week one of my buddies announced that, after a great deal of thought, he had gone in to his supervisors and asked for a lateral transfer that, for all intent and purpose, will deal a death blow to any future promotion. Just a year or so ago, this guy was trying to keep himself on the fast track to promotion and had taken on a great deal of responsibility at his office. He told us that he just realized one day that what he was doing was not good for himself or his family. His job just did not seem that important any more. He valued his relationships over his career. So he took action to take care of those around him in a very specific manner.

My other friend ran for the city council. He is a decent guy with no particular agenda. He just ran a strong campaign and was soundly defeated. He did not hide his head, or whine, or blame anyone else. He took his defeat in stride, and the day after the election, seemed to be just like any other day.

Both of these guys seem to have one thing in common. They put their own needs and egos aside. In today's culture, that basically demands that we always think of ourselves first, and blame others for our shortcomings. These two men, who lead reasonably unceremonious lives, had acted in an extraordinarily courageous manner.

It might be worthwhile to take a moment and reflect on our own lives. In what circumstances do we need to examine the areas where we need to act courageously and go against what our culture expects from us? My two friends did just that and we are all better off because of people like them.

The Deer Stand

Not long ago, Anna Lee and I were in Europe where we went to several churches and cathedrals, not the least of which was the Vatican. While there, we went into the Sistine Chapel. It was crowded, but not to the degree that we were uncomfortable. There were all kinds of signs around that asked for quiet, but every few minutes the crowd would be reminded by a guard asking for silence. In almost every church that we went into, even while people were worshiping, the crowds were noisy and irreverent. OK, now it's time to sound like an old grouchy guy! So many times I go to places right here in our hometown, where people either don't know or don't care that they should just shut up. Go to a museum, a nice restaurant, a concert, a movie or, yes, to a church, and often there is no reverence. Most of the time people just don't get it. There is so much confusion and stimulation in our lives that many people today think that it is natural to live in chaos. When things get too quiet or still, they get uncomfortable and edgy.

That brings to mind deer hunting. It's deer season here in Georgia now, and although I do not deer hunt, many of my friends do. We have not shied-away from their gifts of venison in the past. It makes good chili. Many times these hunters will come in from the woods and talk about how close they feel to God while they are hunting. Part of that is because they are out in the woods and aware of the natural beauty that God has created. It might be, though, that most of that spiritual awareness is brought about because they are quiet. If they are up in a deer stand at 5 a.m., they are silent—sometimes for hours, and guess what, they feel God's presence, often in profound ways.

Silence and reverence are gifts from God. God has given us these gifts so that we may use them to become more aware of His nature and desires for our lives. Let us all figure out a time when we can be still and quiet and listen for God's call on our lives. Let us also recognize that there are times and places where we should just shut the "hell" up! It would do us all good, even an old grouch like me.

Are there times in our day when we seek out silence?

Advice is Cheap

Not too long ago, one of our daughters ran into a little trouble on her job. She asked for some advice and, like a good dad, I was quick to give it. I started with specifics regarding documenting her performance, keeping accurate records, being careful about what she said and to whom, and following the chain of command. All of this advice was well meaning, but in retrospect it was, like most advice, cheap. I had tried to give her specific advice regarding a very narrow set of circumstances. Honestly, my advice to her was with regard to circumstances about which I really did not know very much. After a few days, when things had calmed down a bit, we did have a chance to talk again about her situation. This time I gave her a little more advice, but it was not specific in nature. The advice which I gave my daughter was centered on general principles of behavior. "Be sure you are right. If you know you are right, stand up for yourself. Be firm but not obnoxious. Don't burn any bridges." You get the idea.

My encounter with my daughter is a little bit like our relationship with God. Although God can and does help with specific circumstances, the greatest value of our relationship with Him is our ability to learn basic spiritual principles on which to build our lives. Someone once said that although Jesus healed many people and even raised individuals from the dead, that in the long run, all of these people died anyway. Jesus' ministry was more about our changing our way of life by following Him than it is by His healing the sick. Maybe we should take a minute and examine those spiritual principles around which we build our own lives.

☩

Having a Cocktail With God

We have a friend whose wife died several years ago. This guy has a dynamite story. His father abandoned his family in the teeth of the depression. His mom drove the family across country to California where she started over again. Eventually, our friend carved-out a life of his own in the airline industry. He worked for Hughes aircraft in its heyday (yes, he even saw Howard Hughes during the day from time to time), and eventually became very successful representing airlines in the foreign markets. Our friend has never remarried, and when he speaks of his deceased wife, it is with a wistful twinkle in his eyes. He related one time that each evening throughout their marriage the two of them sat down with one another and had a drink before dinner to celebrate, as he puts it, "having been able to spend one more day together." How cool is that.

So many of our relationships are broken nowadays. There are many reasons, but a primary factor is that our culture encourages us to focus on ourselves and not on our relationships. God is a God Who values relationships. Think of all of the stories in the Christian scriptures that relate to God giving us a glimpse of how we ought to handle our relationships with those that we love and even those that we don't. The prodigal son and the good Samaritan are just two examples that come to mind.

One thing that might be helpful in maintaining our relationships is creating rituals in our lives, like our friend and his wife did, in order to intentionally affirm those that we love and cherish. Maybe we should take a minute and examine our relationships and think of what rituals we might begin that we would cherish years and years from today.

Thinking With the Lower Half
of Our Body

Some people who are important to us in our lives are going through very difficult times. You might say that at this time their life is a calamity. There are many issues involved, but suffice it to say that one of the individuals involved was thinking with the lower half of their body.

What happens when we face calamity in our lives? Some would question why any God would allow these terribly disruptive events to happen in the first place. But we learn as we experience the incredible strength of the very nature of God's love in our own lives, that He has granted us free will and that we could never experience peace without chaos, healing without sickness, strength without weakness, or love without despair. We also realize that much of the calamity that faces us is often due to our own poor decision making or the evil nature of those that have power over us. Although we will never understand or be able to comfortably accept the fact that bad things happen to good people, we can learn from the difficult circumstances that will inevitably face each of us in one way or the other. It may be that facing our deepest trials honestly will allow us to understand on the most basic level what it is that we worship.

Several years ago, Anna Lee and I became owners of the house in which she grew up. It is her family home. The house is located in one of the most beautiful settings in our country. It needed a lot of work and it took a good deal of money to fix it up. We cautioned ourselves at that time that we could not let ourselves begin to "worship" our second home. For the most part, we have been successful. I really believe that dealing, in the very beginning, with the issues regarding where this house should fit in the priorities of our lives, has helped us keep a sense of balance of priorities. This balance may have prevented us from making poor decisions regarding the house that might have led to difficulties later on.

Whether we are dealing with a calamity of our own making, bad luck, or just the daily grind of life that confronts us, we must all come to grips in a moment of gut check honesty what is it that we really worship. It might be worthwhile taking a minute to think about that.

What Are We Going To Do When We Grow Up?

Almost 40 years ago, I was teaching a seminar on career development to graduate students. As part of that class, we had a panel of individuals come in and talk about their own career paths. I can't remember everyone on that panel, but two of the participants made a real impression on me. One of these was a young man just out of college. My brother-in-law, Alvin, had actually taught him economics in a small college the year previous. This young man had become a stock broker, and he told our class that his goal was to become a millionaire before he was thirty. By the way, he did just that. The other man that I remember was a factory worker at a large plant nearby. He told the class about how he had jumped from job to job and that he finally felt that he had landed a job that was steady and secure. I guess what I want to do when I grow up," he said, "is retire." He never made it. He died of a heart attack 30 years later. He was a dear friend named Tim. The most important thing that needs to be said about Tim is that he really "grew up" in a magnificent way. Tim realized that it was not what he was going to "do" when he grew up that was important. Tim understood that it was what he was going to "become" when he grew up that makes all the difference. Tim developed an unbelievably close relationship to God. Tim took great care of his family and friends. He ministered to others in prisons, in his community, and whenever he met anyone, he made time for them in very special ways. When Tim died, he had grown up to become a powerful man of God. He changed many lives for the better, mine included.

What is it that we are going to become when we grow up?

✠

Lessons From Joe Pesci

It's Thanksgiving week and I wonder how many of us are worried to death. When we read the postings of our "friend" on social networking sites, it's amazing how many of us are worried. It might be money, or health, or relationship issues that bother us. Sometimes we worry about assignments that are upcoming, or how we look, or what others think about us. I worry a lot about my family. I really feel a need to "fix" them. I worry too much about organizations with which I am associated and the responsibilities I feel to them. Some people, (of course not I!), actually worry about sports teams that they have become emotionally involved with over the years.

The other night I was watching a movie on TV. I don't remember its name, but Joe Pesci was in it. He played a homeless guy who was giving advice to a more well to do person who was whining about something or the other. Joe's character said something like, "You have a steady job and your wife loves you, so get over it!"

If we are fortunate enough to have a steady job and have anyone who really loves us, we have a great deal to be thankful for. All the rest, as many have said, "is just gravy."

It might be worth taking a minute to think about all that we have to be thankful for and say a prayer for all of those around us who do not have, "a steady job and someone who loves them."

☩

Playing the Lottery

I just told Anna Lee that we need to buy a lottery ticket tonight. I buy about four lottery tickets a year. Tonight I will put down a dollar on the 232 million dollar jackpot that is going to be given away this Friday. I can't be the only one who has fantasized about winning the lottery. I don't fantasize constantly about the lottery, actually, it is only very infrequently that my brain even dwells on the subject, but to be honest, every once in a while I do think what would I do if I won the 232 million or so. I do know a woman who won a little over $500,000 in the lottery. She took home $330,000 after taxes. She told me not long ago that that amount of money changed her life dramatically. She related that she has very few friends from her pre-lottery days. She's not sure why, because all of her money went into the bank. She never missed a day's work, and she and her husband continue to focus on their relationship with their own family. Still, her friends saw her as a different person. It might be that her friends resented the fact that in their eyes she was rewarded without working for it. She had not earned her reward. Her lottery winnings were given, no questions asked, just because she had the winning ticket.

To quote and old song, "That's How It Is With God's Love." It's kind of like winning the lottery. God's love is given, no questions asked, sometimes even before we are aware of His presence in our lives. Not having to earn God's love is a very difficult concept for us to figure out. Often, when we accept God's love for us and allow His Spirit to work in our lives, some people around us back off. Some see us as hypocrites because we have accepted something we have not earned. Some see us as a different person and it makes them uncomfortable.

Accepting God's love takes a tremendous amount of courage because we are frightened that we might have to give up too much of our normal lives. Most of the time that does not happen. God allows us to live abundantly in our old world, but not of our old world. But to be honest, sometimes accepting the free, unearned Love of God is costly, and our lives do change dramatically.

All in all, it is worth the gamble. It is worth taking some time to pray and meditate on what our lives would be like if we actually accepted the Love of God that we can never, ever earn.

A Final Note

There comes a time, in our relationship with God, that we have to stop being theoretical and become personal. I am great at the theoretical. I am interested in theology and have spent a great deal of time talking, thinking, and writing about God. Simply put, that is the easy part. God is God, not for the sake of discussion, but for the sake of personal salvation. A major component of our relation with God must be experienced. True enough we must study and seek to learn about the nature of God, but without the personal experience, all of the rest of our efforts are wasted. My personal experiences with the power of God's love, the truly mountain top experiences, jump to my mind as I look back on my own spiritual journey. There was never a time when I was not in church as a child. I remember the simple, peaceful altar prayer services we had at our home church each Sunday evening. For about 20 minutes the church was darkened, the cross above us was lit, and those who wanted journeyed to the altar to pray. The sounds of familiar hymns softly played on the organ provided a truly prayerful setting. With each Sunday night's service, I was drawn closer and closer to God's presence. One night in particular, I glanced to my right and saw a young girl from our neighborhood who had a terrible reputation, praying with such earnestness that I was overcome with the knowledge that we are all God's children, and that even I was held in a special place in the heart of God.

Fast forward ahead ten years or so. After a decade of sixties doubt and dubious behavior, Anna Lee and I were dealing with the reality that our four year old daughter had type-one diabetes and that she would be giving herself shots each day for the rest of her life. I remember my mother telling Anna Lee and me that we could never believe that God was punishing us or our daughter, Christy, in any way; that God was a God of love. My prayers, during that time, and the experience of feeling God's presence in our lives while our daughter lay so seriously ill, in a very ironic way, was another mountain top experience.

I remember praying so earnestly at the altar of the little country church we joined in the 1970s. I had been handed what seemed to be enormous responsibilities for a 31 year old man, and I felt God's presence and calming in my life, so strongly that I believed that I was undergirded when very challenging problems often confronted me.

Later, there was a particular church retreat when I felt God's presence so strongly that I was awakened in the middle of the night and walked the grounds of our retreat center in prayer and meditation for several hours. I remember at least three other times at very special places, one in complete silence for several days, and one, on a three day spiritual journey in a high security prison. God figuratively knocked me off my feet as I felt Him dealing with the core of my soul. These encounters with God, although not limited to the ones I described, have not come very often in my life. When they have occurred, I have felt God's presence in such mysterious and glorious ways that I have been emotionally overwhelmed.

If I were asked the day and time when I was saved by God and I knew that Jesus was my personal Savior, I would have to say honestly that I do not know. I really don't think pinning that moment down is important for me personally. Do we remember the day that we realized we were loved by our parents? Perhaps some do, I personally do not. I really don't remember the moment that I knew I loved my wife, or even the exact moment that I began to love my children. I believe I have loved my children before they were ever born, and I believe that God has loved me since before I was ever born, and that my love for God and acceptance of Christ has occurred quietly and in some fashion never to be understood. That acceptance has been accentuated by periodic experiences, some of which I have described above, where I get just a notion for the power and mystery and eternal presence of God.

A friend told me one time that our spiritual journey was a lot like breaking a horse. Some horses are broken in very dramatic fashion. Someone jumps on their back and they buck and buck and twist and turn until they realize that they are not going to throw off their rider, so they calm down and accept the rider's presence in their lives. Other horses are broken much more gradually. Someone puts on a bridle and lets the horse get used to that. Then perhaps a blanket, and later still, a saddle are added. One day a rider gently mounts the horse and, without a great deal of thrashing about, the horse is broken. Each horse took different journeys to the same place, but the result was the same for both. They both accepted the rider's presence in their lives.

Thanks for reading these meditations.
Toby Hill—March 2010